P9-EEP-169

Vicki Garrod
July 2005

Birds of Idaho

Field Guide

by Stan Tekiela

ADVENTURE PUBLICATIONS, INC.
CAMBRIDGE, MINNESOTA

TO MY WIFE KATHERINE AND DAUGHTER ABIGAIL
WITH ALL MY LOVE

ACKNOWLEDGMENTS:

Special thanks to Anthony Hertzel for range maps, and Kas Dumroese, co-editor of *A Birder's Guide to Idaho* and subregional editor of *North American Birds*, for reviewing them. Special thanks also to Sandy Livoti for her exceptional eye to detail.

Book design and illustrations by Jonathan Norberg

Photo credits by photographer and page number:

Cover photo: Male Varied Thrush by Steve and Dave Maslowski
Dominique Braud: 260 (adult) **Brian M. Collins**: 160 **Cornell Laboratory of Ornithology**: 62 (female) **Dudley Edmondson**: 10, 12, 16, 18, 20 (soaring), 48 (soaring), 48 (all), 66, 68, 70, 76 (female), 84 (both), 86, 102 (adult), 104, 114 (in flight), 116, 120 (both), 122 (yellow-shafted male), 126, 146 (soaring light morph), 148 (both), 150 (perching light morph), 156, 182 (male), 188, 194 (male), 202 (perching, soaring), 204, 210, 252 (breeding), 262 (male, winter male), 266, 270 (male), 280 **Don Enger**: 44 (rushing, weed dance) **B. Gerlach/DPA***: 236 (male) **Kevin T. Karlson**: 34, 36, 38 (male), 128 (both), 132 (female), 144, 254 (breeding) **Bruce Leventhal**: 258 **Bill Marchel**: 2, 24 (male), 62 (male), 74, 130, 138, 142, 162 (female), 182 (female), 216, 230, 232, 250 **Steve and Dave Maslowski**: 6 (male), 30 (male), 50, 56 (female), 88 (male), 94, 100, 108, 154, 168, 170, 176, 222 (male), 242 (male), 248, 260 (chick-feeding male), 272, 276, 282 **Anthony Mercieca/DPA***: 220 (both), 236 (female) **Steve Mortensen**: 8, 32 (male), 40 (both), 46 (perching), 52, 54, 136, 228, 264 (female), 278 (both) **Warren Nelson**: 122 (yellow-shafted female), 270 (female) **John Pennoyer**: 42, 72, 110, 234, 244 (male) **Brian E. Small**: 6 (female), 26 (breeding and non-breeding males), 28 (both), 30 (male), 38 (winter), 44 (breeding), 56 (male), 58 (both), 60 (both), 64, 76 (Oregon female), 78, 80, 88 (female), 90, 92, 98, 106 (winter), 122 (red-shafted male and female), 132 (male), 134, 140 (both), 158 (male), 164 (perching), 178 (Oregon male), 184, 186, 190 (gray morph), 192, 196 (both), 200, 208, 218 (both), 222 (female), 224, 226, 238, 240, 242 (female), 244 (yellow male), 246, 252 (winter, juvenile), 254 (winter), 262 (female), 268, 274 (all) **Stan Tekiela**: 4 (both), 14, 22 (both), 82, 96 (both), 102 (1 year old), 106 (breeding), 112, 114 (perching), 118, 124, 152, 158 (female), 162 (male), 166, 172, 174, 178 (male), 180, 194 (male), 198, 202 (juvenile), 212, 214, 256 (all), 262 (male) **Brian K. Wheeler**: 20 (perching), 146 (perching light and dark morphs, soaring dark morph, intermediate morph), 150 (perching dark morph, soaring light and dark morphs), 164 (soaring, juvenile), 206 (all) **Jim Zipp**: 190 (brown morph)

*Dembinsky Photo Associates

To the best of the publisher's knowledge, all photos were of live birds.

TABLE OF CONTENTS

Introduction

WHY WATCH BIRDS IN IDAHO?

Millions of people have discovered bird feeding. It's a simple and enjoyable way to bring the beauty of birds closer to your home. Watching birds at your feeder often leads to a lifetime pursuit of bird identification. The *Birds of Idaho Field Guide* is for those who want to identify the common birds of Idaho.

There are over 800 species of birds found in North America. In Idaho alone there have been more than 350 different kinds of birds recorded throughout the years. These bird sightings were diligently recorded by hundreds of bird watchers and became part of the official state record. From these valuable records, I've chosen 122 of the most common birds of Idaho to include in this field guide.

Bird watching, often called birding, is the largest spectator sport in America. Its outstanding popularity in Idaho is due, in part, to an unusually rich and abundant birdlife. Why are there so many birds? One reason is open space. Idaho is over 80,500 square miles (209,300 sq. km), making it the fourteenth largest state. Despite its large size, only about 1.2 million people call Idaho home. On average, that is only 15 people per square mile (6 per sq. km). Most of these people are located in and around only three major cities.

Open space is not the only reason there is such an abundance of birds. It is also the diversity of habitat. Idaho can be broken into three distinct habitats–Rocky Mountains, Columbia Plateau, and Basin and Range Province–each of which supports a different group of birds.

The Rocky Mountains make up more than half of Idaho's entire land mass. Elevations from the lowest valley floor to the tallest peak in the state–Mount Borah–range from approximately 4,000 to 12,650 feet (1,200 to 3,850 m). Located mainly in the central part of the state, the Rockies are home to birds such as Mountain Chickadees and American Dippers.

The Columbia Plateau lies in the southern part of the state just south of the Rocky Mountains. It is a diverse area, with the Snake River Plain making up most of its features. This wide river plain is the most inhabited region in Idaho and is home to birds such as Mountain Bluebirds and Green-tailed Towhees.

Within the Columbia Plateau is a small region called the Basin and Range Province. Elevations here range from 4,000 to 6,000 feet (1,200 to 1,850 m). With its many valleys and rivers, this area is mostly agricultural. It is a good place to see such birds as Lark Sparrows and California Quail.

Idaho also has more than 20.4 million acres (8.2 million ha) of national forestland. Ruffed Grouse, Cooper's Hawks and many other bird species are attracted to these richly wooded reserves.

There are many large lakes in Idaho, most of which are located in the Panhandle. One of these is Lake Pend Oreille. Covering 133 square miles (346 sq. km), it is the state's largest lake. Rivers that swell with snowmelt from the Rocky Mountains feed Idaho lakes each spring. Idaho also has many reservoirs. Water birds such as Pied-billed Grebes and Western Grebes are attracted to these bodies of water.

Not only does Idaho have varying habitats, it also has variations in the weather. Since the state extends over 480 miles (773 km) from north to south, the weather ranges greatly. The Rockies in central Idaho create a moisture barrier, which results in a rain shadow effect in southern Idaho, making it much drier there. Southwestern Idaho is the warmest part of the state, while the Panhandle in the northwest is the coldest.

Whatever the elevation or weather, there are birds to watch in each season. Whether witnessing a migration of hawks in the fall or welcoming back hummingbirds in spring, there is variety and excitement in birding as each season turns to the next.

OBSERVE WITH A STRATEGY; TIPS FOR IDENTIFYING BIRDS

Identifying birds isn't as difficult as you might think. By simply following a few basic strategies, you can increase your chances of successfully identifying most birds you see! One of the first and easiest things to do when you see a new bird is to note its color. (Also, since this book is organized by color, you will go right to that color section to find it.)

Next, note the size of the bird. A strategy to quickly estimate size is to select a small-, medium- and large-sized bird to use for reference. For example, most people are familiar with robins. A robin, measured from tip of the bill to tip of the tail, is 10 inches (25 cm) long. Using the robin as an example of a medium-sized bird, select two other birds, one smaller and one larger. Many people use a House Sparrow, at about 6 inches (15 cm), and an American Crow, about 18 inches (45 cm). When you see a bird that you don't know, you can quickly ask yourself, "Is it smaller than a robin, but larger than a sparrow?" When you look in your field guide to help identify your bird, you'll know it's roughly between 6 and 10 inches (15 to 25 cm) long. This will help to narrow your choices.

Next, note the size, shape and color of the bill. Is it long, short, thick, thin, pointed, blunt, curved or straight? Seed-eating birds, such as Evening Grosbeaks, have bills that are thick and strong enough to crack even the toughest seeds. Birds that sip nectar, such as Rufous Hummingbirds, need long thin bills to reach deep into flowers. Hawks and owls tear their prey with very sharp, curving bills. Sometimes, just noting the bill shape can help you decide if the bird is a woodpecker, finch, grosbeak, blackbird or bird of prey.

Next, take a look around and note the habitat in which you see the bird. Is it wading in a marsh? Walking along a riverbank? Soaring in the sky? Is it perched high in the trees or hopping along the forest floor? Because of their preferences in diet and habitat, you'll usually see robins hopping on the ground, but not often eating the seeds at your feeder. Or you'll see a Black-headed Grosbeak sitting on a branch of a tree, but not climbing down the tree trunk headfirst the way a nuthatch does.

Noticing what a bird is eating will give you another clue to help you identify that bird. Feeding is a big part of any bird's life. Fully one-third of all bird activity revolves around searching for and catching food, or actually eating. While birds don't always follow all the rules of what we think they eat, you can make some general assumptions. Northern Flickers, for instance, feed upon ants and other insects, so you wouldn't expect to see them visiting a backyard feeder. Some birds, such as Barn Swallows and Cliff Swallows, feed upon flying insects, and spend hours swooping and diving to catch a meal.

Sometimes you can identify a bird by the way it perches. Body posture can help you differentiate between an American Crow and a Red-tailed Hawk. American Crows lean forward over their feet on a branch, while hawks perch in a vertical position. Look for this the next time you see a large unidentified bird in a tree.

Birds in flight are often difficult to identify, but noting the size and shape of the wing will help. A bird's wing size is in direct proportion to its body size, weight and type of flying. The shape of the wing determines if the bird flies fast and with precision, or slowly and less precisely. Birds such as House Finches, which flit around in thick tangles of branches, have short round wings. Birds that soar on warm updrafts of air, such as Turkey Vultures, have long broad wings. Barn Swallows have short pointed wings that slice through air, propelling their swift and accurate flight.

Some birds have unique flight patterns that aid in identification. American Goldfinches fly in a distinctive up-and-down pattern that makes it look as if they are riding a roller coaster.

While it's not easy to make these observations in the short time you often have to watch a "mystery bird," practicing these methods of identification will greatly expand your skills in birding. Also, seek the guidance of a more experienced birder who will help you improve your skills and answer questions on the spot.

BIRD BASICS

It's easier to identify birds and communicate about them if you know the names of the different parts of a bird. For instance, it's more effective to use the word "crest" to indicate the set of extra long feathers on top of the head of a Steller's Jay than to try to describe it.

The following illustration points out the basic parts of a bird. Because it is a composite of many birds, it shouldn't be confused with any actual bird.

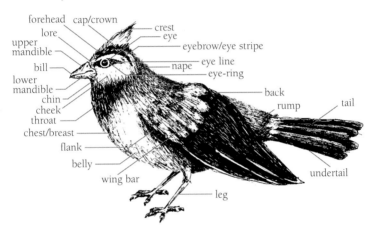

Bird Color Variables

No other animal has a color pallet like a bird's. Brilliant blues, lemon yellows, showy reds and iridescent greens are common-place within the bird world. In general, the male birds are more colorful than their female counterparts. This is probably to help the male attract a mate, essentially saying, "Hey, look at me!" It also calls attention to the male's overall health. The better the condition of his feathers, the better his food source and territory, and therefore the better his potential for a mate.

Female birds that don't look like their male counterparts (such species are called sexually dimorphic, meaning "two forms") are often a nondescript color, as seen with the Lazuli Bunting. These muted tones help hide the females during weeks of motionless incubation, and draw less attention to them when they are out feeding or taking a break from the rigors of raising their young.

In some species, such as the Bald Eagle, Steller's Jay and Downy Woodpecker, the male birds look nearly identical to the females. In the case of the woodpeckers, the sexes are only differentiated by a single red or sometimes yellow mark. Depending on the species, the mark may be on top of the head, face, nape of the neck or just behind the bill.

During the first year, juvenile birds often look like the mothers. Since brightly colored feathers are used mainly for attracting a mate, young non-breeding males don't have a need for colorful plumage. It is not until the first spring molt (or several years later, depending on the species) that young males obtain their breeding colors.

Both breeding and winter plumages are the result of molting. Molting is the process of dropping old worn feathers and replacing them with new ones. All birds molt, typically twice a year, with the spring molt usually occurring in late winter. During this time, most birds produce their breeding plumage (brighter colors for attracting mates), which lasts throughout the summer.

Winter plumage is the result of the late summer molt, which serves a couple of important functions. First, it adds feathers for warmth in the coming winter. Second, in some species it produces feathers that tend to be drab in color, which helps to camouflage the birds and hide them from predators. The winter plumage of the male American Goldfinch, for example, is an olive brown, unlike its obvious canary yellow color in summer. Luckily for us, some birds, such as Lewis's Woodpeckers, retain their bright summer colors all year long.

BIRD NESTS

Bird nests are truly an amazing feat of engineering. Imagine building your home strong enough to weather a storm, large enough to hold your entire family, insulated enough to shelter them from cold and heat, and waterproof enough to keep out rain. Now, build it without any blueprints or directions, and without the use of your hands or feet! Birds do!

Before building a nest, an appropriate site must be selected. In some species, such as House Wrens, the male picks out several potential sites and assembles several small twigs in each. This discourages other birds from using nearby nest cavities. These "extra" nests are occasionally called dummy nests. The female is then taken around and shown all the choices. She chooses her favorite and finishes constructing the nest. In some other species of birds–the Bullock's Oriole, for example–it is the female who chooses the site and builds the nest with the male offering only an occasional suggestion. Each species has its own nest-building routine, which is strictly followed.

Nesting material usually consists of natural elements found in the immediate area. Most nests consist of plant fibers (such as bark peeled from grapevines), sticks, mud, dried grass, feathers, fur, or soft fuzzy tufts from thistle. Some birds, including Broad-tailed Hummingbirds, use spider webs to glue nesting materials together. Nesting material is limited to what a bird can hold or carry. Because of this, a bird must make many trips afield to gather enough materials to complete its nest. Most nests take at least four days or more, and hundreds, if not thousands, of trips to build.

As you'll see in the following illustrations, birds build a wide variety of nest types.

ground nest   platform nest   cup nest   pendulous nest

The simple **ground nest** is scraped out of the earth. A shallow depression that usually contains no nesting material, it is made by birds such as the Killdeer and Horned Lark.

Another kind of nest, the **platform nest**, represents a more complex type of nest building. Constructed of small twigs and branches, the platform nest is a simple arrangement of sticks which forms a platform and features a small depression to nestle the eggs.

Some platform nests, such as those of the Canada Goose, are constructed on the ground and are made with mud and grass. Platform nests can also be on cliffs, bridges, balconies or even in flowerpots. This kind of nest gives space to adventurous young-sters and functions as a landing platform for the parents. Many waterfowl construct platform nests on the ground, usually near water or actually in the water. These floating platform nests vary with the water level, thus preventing nests with eggs from being flooded. Platform nests, constructed by such birds as Mourning Doves and herons, are not anchored to the tree and may tumble from the branches during high winds and storms.

The **cup nest** is a modified platform nest, used by three-quarters of all songbirds. Constructed from the outside in, a supporting platform is constructed first. This platform is attached firmly to a tree, shrub or rock ledge. Next, the sides are constructed of grasses, small twigs, bark or leaves, which are woven together and often glued with mud for additional strength. The inner cup, lined with feathers, animal fur, soft plant material or animal hair, is constructed last. The mother bird uses her chest to cast the final contours of the inner nest.

The **pendulous nest** is an unusual nest, looking more like a sock hanging from a branch than a nest. Inaccessible to most predators, these nests are attached to the ends of the smallest branches of a tree, and often wave wildly in the breeze. Woven very tightly of plant fibers, they are strong and watertight, taking up to a week to build. More commonly used by tropical birds, this complicated nest type has also been mastered by orioles and kinglets. A small opening on the top or side allows the parents access to the grass-lined interior. (It must be one heck of a ride to be inside one of these nests during a windy spring thunderstorm!)

One of the most clever of all nest types is known as the **no nest** or daycare nest. Parasitic birds, such as Brown-headed Cowbirds, build no nests at all! The egg-laden female expertly searches out other birds' nests and sneaks in to lay one of her own eggs while the host mother is not looking, thereby leaving the host mother to raise an adopted youngster. The mother cowbird wastes no energy building a nest only to have it raided by a predator. By using several nests of other birds, she spreads out her progeny so at least one of her offspring will live to maturity.

Another type of nest, the **cavity nest**, is used by many birds, including woodpeckers and Western Bluebirds. The cavity nest is usually excavated in a tree branch or trunk and offers shelter from storms, sun, predators and cold. A relatively small entrance hole in a tree leads to an inner chamber up to 10 inches (25 cm) below. Usually constructed by woodpeckers, the cavity nest is typically used only once by its builder, but subsequently can be used for many years by birds such as mergansers, Tree Swallows and bluebirds, which do not have the capability of excavating one for themselves. Kingfishers, on the other hand, excavate a tunnel up to 4 feet (1 m) long, which connects the entrance in a riverbank to the nest chamber. These cavity nests are often sparsely lined because they are already well insulated.

Some birds, including some swallows, take nest building one step further. They use a collection of small balls of mud to construct an adobe-style home. Constructed beneath the eaves of houses, under bridges or inside chimneys, some of these nests look like simple cup nests. Others are completely enclosed, with small tunnel-like openings that lead into a safe nesting chamber for the baby birds.

WHO BUILDS THE NEST?

In general, the female bird builds the nest. She gathers nesting materials and constructs a nest, with an occasional visit from her mate to check on the progress. In some species, both parents contribute equally to the construction of a nest. A male bird might forage for precisely the right sticks, grass or mud, but it's often the female that forms or puts together the nest. She uses her body to form the egg chamber. Rarely does the male build a nest by himself.

FLEDGING

Fledging is the interval between hatching and flight or leaving the nest. Some birds leave the nest within hours of hatching (precocial), but it might be weeks before they are able to fly. This is common with waterfowl and shorebirds. Until they start to fly, they are called fledglings. Birds that are still in the nest are called nestlings. Other baby birds are born naked and blind, and remain in the nest for several weeks (altricial).

WHY BIRDS MIGRATE

Why do birds migrate? The short answer is simple–food. Birds migrate to areas with high concentrations of food, as it is easier to breed where food is than where it is not. A typical migrating bird–the Rose-breasted Grosbeak, for instance–migrates from the tropics of Central and South America to nest in the forests of North America, taking advantage of billions of newly hatched insects to feed its young. This trip is called **complete migration**.

Some birds of prey return from their complete migration to northern regions that are overflowing with small rodents, such as mice and voles, that have continued to breed in winter.

Complete migrators have a set time and pattern of migration. Each year at nearly the same time, they take off and head for a specific wintering ground. Complete migrators may travel great distances, sometimes as much as 15,000 miles (24,150 km) or more in a year. But complete migration doesn't necessarily imply flying from the cold, frozen northland to a tropical destination. The Dark-eyed Junco, for example, is a complete migrator that flies from the far reaches of Canada to spend the winter right here in Idaho.

There are many interesting aspects to complete migrators. In the spring, males usually migrate several weeks before the females, arriving early to scope out possibilities for nesting sites and food sources, and to begin to defend territories. The females arrive several weeks later. In the autumn, in many species, the females and their young leave early, often up to four weeks before the adult males.

All migrators are not the same type. There are **partial migrators**, such as American Goldfinches, that usually wait until the food supply dwindles before flying south. Unlike complete migrators, the partial migrators move only far enough south, or sometimes east and west, to find abundant food. In some years it might be only a few hundred miles, while in other years it might be nearly a thousand. This kind of migration, dependent on the weather and available food, is sometimes called **seasonal movement**.

Unlike the predictable ebbing and flowing behavior of complete migrators or partial migrators, **irruptive migrators** can move every third to fifth year or, in some cases, in consecutive years. These migrations are triggered when times are really tough and food is scarce. Red-breasted Nuthatches are a good example of irruptive migrators, because they leave their normal northern range in search of food or in response to overpopulation.

How Do Birds Migrate?

One of the many secrets of migration is fat. While we humans are fighting the battle of the bulge, birds intentionally gorge themselves to put on as much fat as possible while still being able to fly. Fat provides the greatest amount of energy per unit of weight, and in the same way that your car needs gas, birds are propelled by fat and stalled without it.

During long migratory flights, fat deposits are used up quickly, and birds need to stop to "refuel." This is when backyard bird feeding stations and undeveloped, natural spaces around our towns and cities are especially important. Some birds require up to two to three days of constant feeding to build up their fat reserves before continuing their seasonal trip.

Some birds, such as most eagles, hawks, ospreys, falcons and vultures, migrate during the day. Larger birds can hold more body fat, go longer without eating and take longer to migrate. These birds glide along on rising columns of warm air, called thermals, which hold them aloft while they slowly make their way north or south. They generally rest at night and hunt early in the morning before the sun has a chance to warm up the land and create good soaring conditions. Birds migrating during the day use a combination of landforms, rivers, and the rising and setting sun to guide them in the right direction.

Most other birds migrate during the night. Studies show that some birds which migrate at night use the stars to navigate. Others use the setting sun, while still others, such as doves, use the earth's magnetic fields to guide them north or south. While flying at night might seem like a crazy idea, nocturnal migration is safer for several reasons. First, there are fewer nighttime predators for migrating birds. Second, traveling at night allows time during the day to find food in unfamiliar surroundings. Finally, nighttime wind patterns tend to be flat, or laminar. These flat winds don't have the turbulence associated with the daytime winds and can actually help carry smaller birds by pushing them along.

HOW TO USE THIS GUIDE

To help you quickly and easily identify birds, this book is organized by color. Simply note the color of the bird and turn to that section. Refer to the first page for the color key. The Red-naped Sapsucker, for example, is black and white with red on its head. Because the bird is mostly black and white, it will be found in the black and white section. Each color section is also arranged by size, generally with smaller birds first. Sections may also incorporate the average size in a range, which, in some cases, reflects size differences between male and female birds. Flip through the pages in that color section to find the bird. If you already know the name of the bird, check the index for the page number. In some species, the male and female are remarkably different in color. In these cases, the opposite sex is shown in a smaller inset photograph with a page reference. These birds, therefore, will be found in two different color sections.

In the description section you will find a variety of information about the bird. On the next page is a sample of the information included in the book.

RANGE MAPS

Range maps are included for each bird. Colored areas indicate where in the state a particular bird is most likely to be found. Green is used for summer, blue for winter, red for year-round and yellow for areas where the bird is seen during migration. While every effort has been made to accurately depict these ranges, they are only general guidelines. Ranges actually change on an ongoing basis due to a variety of factors. Changes in weather, species abundance, landscape and vital resources such as the availability of food and water can affect local populations, migration and movements, causing birds to be found in areas that are atypical for the species.

Colored areas simply mean bird sightings for that species have been frequent in those areas and less frequent in the others. Please use the maps as intended–as general guides only.

COMMON NAME
Scientific name

COLOR INDICATOR

YEAR-ROUND
MIGRATION
SUMMER
WINTER

Size: measures head to tail, may include wingspan

Male: a brief description of the male bird, and may include breeding, winter or other plumages

Female: a brief description of the female bird, which is sometimes not the same as the male

Juvenile: a brief description of the juvenile bird, which often looks like the female

Nest: the kind of nest this bird builds to raise its young; who builds the nest; how many broods per year

Eggs: how many eggs you might expect to see in a nest; color and marking

Incubation: the average time parents spend incubating the eggs; who does the incubation

Fledging: the average time young spend in the nest after hatching but before they leave the nest; who does the most "childcare" and feeding

Migration: complete (consistent, seasonal), partial migrator (seasonal, destination varies), irruptive (unpredictable, depends on the food supply), non-migrator; additional comments

Food: what the bird eats most of the time (e.g., seeds, insects, fruit, nectar, small mammals, fish); if it typically comes to a bird feeding station

Compare: notes about other birds that look similar, and the pages on which they can be found

Stan's Notes: Interesting gee-whiz natural history information. This could be something to look or listen for, or something to help positively identify the bird. Also includes remarkable features.

female pg. 105

male

BROWN-HEADED COWBIRD
Molothrus ater

Size: 7½" (19 cm)

Male: A glossy black bird, reminiscent of a Red-winged Blackbird. Chocolate brown head with a pointed, sharp gray bill.

Female: dull brown bird with bill similar to male

Juvenile: similar to female, only dull gray color and a streaked chest

Nest: no nest; lays eggs in nests of other birds

Eggs: 5-7; white with brown markings

Incubation: 10-13 days; host bird incubates eggs

Fledging: 10-11 days; host birds feed young

Migration: complete, to southern states

Food: insects, seeds; will come to seed feeders

Compare: The male Red-winged Blackbird (pg. 9) is slightly larger, with red and yellow patches on upper wings. European Starling (pg. 5) has a shorter tail.

Stan's Notes: A member of the blackbird family. Of approximately 750 species of parasitic birds worldwide, this is the only parasitic bird in the state, laying eggs in host birds' nests, leaving others to raise its young. Cowbirds are known to have laid eggs in nests of over 200 species of birds. Some birds reject cowbird eggs, but most incubate them and raise the young, even to the exclusion of their own. Look for warblers and other birds feeding young birds twice their own size. At one time cowbirds followed bison to feed on insects attracted to the animals.

winter

breeding

EUROPEAN STARLING
Sturnus vulgaris

YEAR-ROUND

Size: 7½" (19 cm)

Male: Gray-to-black bird with white speckles in fall and winter. Shiny purple black during spring and summer. Long, pointed yellow bill in spring turns gray in fall. Short tail.

Female: same as male

Juvenile: similar to adult, gray brown in color with a streaked chest

Nest: cavity; male and female line the cavity; 2 broods per year

Eggs: 4-6; bluish with brown markings

Incubation: 12-14 days; female and male incubate

Fledging: 18-20 days; female and male feed young

Migration: non-migrator to partial migrator; some will move to southern states

Food: insects, seeds, fruit; comes to seed and suet feeders

Compare: Male Brown-headed Cowbird (pg. 3) has a brown head and longer tail.

Stan's Notes: A great songster, this bird can also mimic sounds. Often displaces woodpeckers, chickadees and other cavity-nesting birds. Can be very aggressive and destroy eggs or young of other birds. The bill changes color with the seasons: yellow in spring and gray in autumn. Jaws are designed to be the most powerful when opening, as they pry open crevices to locate hidden insects. Gathers in the hundreds in autumn. Not a native bird, it was introduced to New York City in 1890-91 from Europe.

male

female

SPOTTED TOWHEE
Pipilo maculatus

Size: 8½" (22 cm)

Male: A mostly black bird with dirty red-brown sides and white belly. Multiple white spots on wings and sides. Long black tail with a white tip. Rich red eyes.

Female: very similar to male, with a brown head

Juvenile: brown with a heavily streaked chest

Nest: cup; female builds; 1-2 broods per year

Eggs: 3-5; white with brown markings

Incubation: 12-14 days; female and male incubate

Fledging: 10-12 days; female and male feed young

Migration: partial migrator to non-migrator

Food: seeds, fruit, insects

Compare: Closely related to the Green-tailed Towhee (pg. 225), which appears nothing like the bold black and red of the Spotted Towhee.

YEAR-ROUND
SUMMER

Stan's Notes: Not as common as the Green-tailed Towhee, but it inhabits a similar habitat. Found in a variety of habitats, from thick brush and forest edges to suburban backyards. Often heard noisily scratching around through dead leaves on the ground in search of food. Over 70 percent of its diet is plant material, consuming more insects in the spring and summer. Well known for retreating from danger by walking away rather than taking to flight. Female builds nest, nearly always on the ground beneath bushes, but away from where the male perches to sing. Begins breeding in April, with egg laying occurring in May. After breeding season, it moves to higher elevations. Song and plumage vary geographically and are not well studied or understood.

female pg. 111

male

RED-WINGED BLACKBIRD
Agelaius phoeniceus

Size: 8½" (22 cm)

Male: Jet black bird with red and yellow shoulder patches on upper wings. Pointed black bill.

Female: heavily streaked brown bird with a pointed brown bill and white eyebrows

Juvenile: same as female

Nest: cup; female builds; 2-3 broods per year

Eggs: 3-4; bluish green with brown markings

Incubation: 10-12 days; female incubates

Fledging: 11-14 days; female and male feed young

Migration: partial migrator to non-migrator; will move around the state to find food in winter

Food: seeds, insects; will come to seed feeders

Compare: Slightly larger than the male Brown-headed Cowbird (pg. 3), but is less iridescent and lacks Cowbird's brown head. Differs from all blackbirds due to the red and yellow patches on its wings (epaulets).

Stan's Notes: One of the most widespread and numerous birds in Idaho. It is a sure sign of spring when the Red-winged Blackbirds return to the marshes. Flocks of up to 100,000 birds have been reported. Males return before the females and defend territories by singing from tops of surrounding vegetation. Males repeat call from the tops of cattails while showing off their red and yellow wing bars (epaulets). Females choose mate and usually will nest over shallow water in thick stands of cattails. Red-wingeds feed mostly on seeds in fall and spring, switching to insects during summer.

female pg. 113

male

BREWER'S BLACKBIRD
Euphagus cyanocephalus

YEAR-ROUND
SUMMER

Size: 9" (22.5 cm)

Male: Overall glossy black, shining green in direct light. Head more purple than green. Bright white or pale yellow eyes. Winter plumage can be dull gray to black.

Female: similar to male, only overall grayish brown, most have dark eyes

Juvenile: similar to female

Nest: cup; female builds; 1-2 broods per year

Eggs: 4-6; gray with brown markings

Incubation: 12-14 days; female incubates

Fledging: 13-14 days; female and male feed young

Migration: non-migrator to partial migrator in Idaho

Food: insects, seeds, fruit

Compare: The male Brown-headed Cowbird (pg. 3) is smaller and has a brown head. Male Red-winged Blackbird (pg. 9) has obvious red and yellow shoulder marks.

Stan's Notes: Common blackbird often found in association with agricultural lands and seen in open areas such as wet pastures and mountain meadows up to 10,000 feet (3,050 m). Male and some females are easily identified by their bright, nearly white eyes. It will usually nest in a shrub, small tree or directly on the ground. Prefers to nest in small colonies of up to 20 pairs. Will flock with other blackbird family members such as Red-wingeds and cowbirds. A common cowbird host. Gathers in large flocks for fall migration. It is expanding its range in North America.

female pg. 117

male

SUMMER

YELLOW-HEADED BLACKBIRD
Xanthocephalus xanthocephalus

Size: 9-11" (22.5-28 cm)

Male: Large black bird with a lemon yellow head, chest and nape of neck. Black mask and a gray bill. White wing patches.

Female: similar to male, only slightly smaller with a brown body, dull yellow head and chest

Juvenile: similar to female

Nest: cup; female builds; 2 broods per year

Eggs: 3-5; greenish white with brown markings

Incubation: 11-13 days; female incubates

Fledging: 9-12 days; female feeds young

Migration: complete, to southern states and Mexico

Food: insects, seeds

Compare: Larger than the male Red-winged Blackbird (pg. 9), which has red and yellow patches on its wings. Male Yellow-headed Blackbird is the only large black bird with a bright yellow head.

Stan's Notes: Usually heard before seen, Yellow-headed Blackbird has a low, hoarse, raspy or metallic call. Nests in deep water marshes unlike its cousin, the Red-winged Blackbird, which prefers shallow water. The male gives an impressive mating display, flying with head drooped and feet and tail pointing down while steadily beating its wings. The female incubates alone and feeds between three to five young. Young keep low and out of sight for up to three weeks before starting to fly. Migrates in flocks of up to 200 with other blackbirds. Flocks made up mainly of males return first in early April; females return later. Most colonies consist of 20 to 100 nests.

AMERICAN COOT
Fulica americana

YEAR-ROUND
SUMMER

Size: 13-16" (33-40 cm)

Male: Slate gray to black all over, white bill with dark band near tip. Green legs and feet. A small white patch near the base of the tail. Prominent red eyes, with a small red patch above bill between eyes.

Female: same as male

Juvenile: much paler than adult, with a gray bill and same white rump patch

Nest: floating platform; female and male build; 1 brood per year

Eggs: 9-12; pinkish buff with brown markings

Incubation: 21-25 days; female and male incubate

Fledging: 49-52 days; female and male feed young

Migration: partial migrator to complete, along western coastal U.S. and Mexico, Central America

Food: insects, aquatic plants

Compare: Smaller than most waterfowl, it is the only black water bird or duck-like bird with a white bill.

Stan's Notes: An excellent diver and swimmer, often seen in large flocks on open water. Not a duck, as it doesn't have webbed feet, but instead has large lobed toes. When taking off, scrambles across surface of water with wings flapping. Bobs head while swimming. Nest is floating mat of vegetation. Huge flocks of up to 1,000 birds gather for fall migration. The unusual name is of unknown origin, but in Middle English, the word *coote* was used to describe various waterfowl–perhaps it stuck. Also called Mud Hen.

AMERICAN CROW
Corvus brachyrhynchos

YEAR-ROUND

Size:	18" (45 cm)
Male:	All-black bird with black bill, legs and feet. Can have a purple sheen in direct sunlight.
Female:	same as male
Juvenile:	same as adult
Nest:	platform; female builds; 1 brood per year
Eggs:	4-6; bluish to olive green, brown markings
Incubation:	18 days; female incubates
Fledging:	28-35 days; female and male feed young
Migration:	non-migrator to partial migrator
Food:	fruit, insects, mammals, fish, carrion; will come to seed and suet feeders
Compare:	Similar to the Common Raven (pg. 19), but has a smaller bill and lacks shaggy throat feathers. Crow has higher-pitched call than the Raven's deep, low raspy call. Crow has a squared tail. Raven has a wedge-shaped tail, apparent in flight. Black-billed Magpie (pg. 43) has a long tail and white belly.

Stan's Notes: One of the most recognizable birds in Idaho. Often reuses its nest every year if not taken over by a Great Horned Owl. Collects and stores bright, shiny objects in the nest. Able to mimic other birds and human voices. One of the smartest of all birds and very social, often entertaining itself by provoking chases with other birds. Feeds on road kill but is rarely hit by cars. Can live up to 20 years. Unmated birds, known as helpers, help raise young. Large extended families roost together at night, dispersing during the day to hunt.

COMMON RAVEN
Corvus corax

YEAR-ROUND

Size: 22-27" (56-69 cm)

Male: Large all-black bird with a large black bill, a shaggy beard of feathers on the chin and throat, and a large wedge-shaped tail, seen in flight.

Female: same as male

Juvenile: same as adult

Nest: platform; female and male build; 1 brood per year

Eggs: 4-6; pale green with brown markings

Incubation: 18-21 days; female incubates

Fledging: 38-44 days; female and male feed young

Migration: non-migrator to partial migrator

Food: insects, fruit, small animals, carrion

Compare: Larger than its cousin, the American Crow (pg. 17), which lacks the throat patch of feathers. Glides on flat outstretched wings, compared to the slightly V-shaped pattern of Crow. Low raspy call distinguishes the Raven from the higher-pitched Crow.

Stan's Notes: Considered by some to be the smartest of all birds. Known for its aerial acrobatics and long swooping dives. Scavenges with crows and gulls. Known to follow wolf packs around to pick up scraps and pick at bones of a kill. Complex courtship includes grabbing bills, preening each other and cooing. Mates for life. Uses same nest site for many years. Most don't breed until 3 to 4 years of age.

soaring

TURKEY VULTURE
Cathartes aura

Size: 26-32" (66-80 cm); up to 6-foot wingspan

Male: Large bird with obvious red head and legs. In flight, the wings appear two-toned: black leading edge with gray on the trailing edge and tip. The tips of wings end in finger-like projections. Long squared tail. Ivory bill.

Female: same as male

Juvenile: similar to adult, with gray-to-blackish head and bill

Nest: no nest, or minimal nest on cliff or in cave; 1 brood per year

Eggs: 2; white with brown markings

Incubation: 38-41 days; female and male incubate

Fledging: 66-88 days; female and male feed young

Migration: complete, to southern states, Mexico, and Central and South America

Food: carrion, just about any dead animal of any size; parents regurgitate for young

Compare: Smaller than the Bald Eagle (pg. 49), look for Vulture's two-toned wings. Flies holding wings in a slight V shape, unlike the Eagle's straight wing position.

Stan's Notes: The vulture's naked head is an adaptation to reduce risk of feather fouling (picking up diseases) from carcasses. Unlike hawks and eagles, it has weak feet more suited to walking than grasping. One of the few birds that has a developed sense of smell. Mostly mute, making only grunts and groans. Seen in trees with wings outstretched to catch sun.

drying

DOUBLE-CRESTED CORMORANT
Phalacrocorax auritus

Size: 33" (84 cm)

Male: Large all-black water bird with long snake-like neck. A long yellow orange bill with a hooked tip.

Female: same as male

Juvenile: lighter brown with a grayish-colored breast and neck

Nest: platform, in colony; male and female build; 1 brood per year

Eggs: 3-4; bluish white without markings

Incubation: 25-29 days; female and male incubate

Fledging: 37-42 days; male and female feed young

Migration: complete, to western coastal U.S., southern states, Mexico and Central America

Food: small fish, aquatic insects

Compare: Similar size as the Turkey Vulture (pg. 21), which also perches on branches with wings open to dry in sun, but Vulture has a naked red head. Twice the size of American Coot (pg. 15), which lacks the Cormorant's long neck and long pointed bill.

Stan's Notes: Often seen flying in large V formation. Often roosts in large groups in trees near water. Catches fish by swimming with wings held at its sides. To dry off it strikes an erect pose with wings outstretched, facing the sun. The name refers to its nearly invisible crests. "Cormorant" comes from the Latin *corvus*, meaning "crow," and *L. marinus*, meaning "pertaining to the sea," literally, "Sea Crow."

male

female

DOWNY WOODPECKER
Picoides pubescens

YEAR-ROUND

Size: 6" (15 cm)

Male: A small woodpecker with an all-white belly, black-and-white spotted wings, a black line running through the eyes, a short black bill, a white stripe down the back and red mark on the back of the head. Several small black spots along the sides of white tail.

Female: same as male, but lacks a red mark on head

Juvenile: same as female, some have a red mark near the forehead

Nest: cavity; male and female excavate; 1 brood per year

Eggs: 3-5; white without markings

Incubation: 11-12 days; female and male incubate, the female during day, male at night

Fledging: 20-25 days; male and female feed young

Migration: non-migrator

Food: insects, seeds; visits seed and suet feeders

Compare: Almost identical to the Hairy Woodpecker (pg. 33), but smaller. Look for the shorter, thinner bill of Downy to differentiate them.

Stan's Notes: Abundant and widespread where trees are present. Stiff tail feathers help brace it like a tripod as it clings to a tree. Like all woodpeckers, it has a long barbed tongue to pull insects from tiny places. Male and female will drum on branches or hollow logs to announce territories, which are rarely larger than 5 acres (2 ha). Male performs most brooding. Will winter roost in cavity. Doesn't breed in high elevations, but often moves there in winter for food.

female pg. 93

breeding male

non-breeding male

SUMMER

LARK BUNTING
Calamospiza melanocorys

Size: 6½" (16 cm)

Male: Short, stocky black bird with a large broad head, white wing patches and large bluish gray bill. Winter is black, brown, gray and white-striped, with white wing patches.

Female: overall brown with a heavily streaked chest, white belly, black vertical line on each side of white chin, may have a dark central spot on the chest, faint white eyebrows

Juvenile: similar to adult of the same sex

Nest: cup; female builds; 1-2 broods per year

Eggs: 4-6; pale blue with markings

Incubation: 11-13 days; female and male incubate

Fledging: 8-12 days; female and male feed young

Migration: complete, to southwestern states, Mexico

Food: insects, seeds

Compare: The breeding male's bold black and white plumage is hard to confuse with any other bird's. Look for the rather large broad head and large bill to help identify.

Stan's Notes: Common in eastern and southern parts of Idaho in dry plains and sagebrush regions. Has short rounded wings. Flying with shallow wing beats, the male flashes white wing patches. Male takes to air to display to female, setting its wings in a V position and floating back, rocking like a butterfly, singing a most amazing song. Song is like the song of Old World larks, hence the common name. Will flock with hundreds, if not thousands, of other Lark Buntings in autumn for migration.

male

female

SUMMER

RED-NAPED SAPSUCKER
Sphyrapicus nuchalis

Size: 8½" (22 cm)

Male: Black-and-white pattern on the back in two rows. Red forehead, chin and nape of neck.

Female: same as male, but has white chin and more white on back

Juvenile: brown version of adults, lacking any of the red markings

Nest: cavity; the male and female build; 1 brood per year

Eggs: 3-7; pale white without markings

Incubation: 12-13 days; female and male incubate

Fledging: 25-29 days; female and male feed young

Migration: complete, to Mexico and Central America

Food: insects, tree sap

Compare: The Lewis's Woodpecker (pg. 227) lacks the Red-naped's black-and-white pattern. The male Williamson's Sapsucker (pg. 31) has a bright yellow belly.

Stan's Notes: Summers in Idaho. Closely related to Yellow-bellied Sapsuckers of the eastern U.S. Often associated with aspen, willow and cottonwood trees, nearly always nesting in aspen trees where they are present. Creates several horizontal rows of holes in a tree from which sap oozes. A wide variety of birds and animals use the sap wells that sapsuckers drill. Sapsuckers lap the sap and eat the insects that are also attracted to sap. Can't suck sap as the name implies; rather, they lap it with their tongues. Some females lack the white chin that helps to differentiate the sexes.

female

male

MIGRATION
SUMMER

WILLIAMSON'S SAPSUCKER
Sphyrapicus thyroideus

Size: 9" (22.5 cm)

Male: More black than white with a red chin and bright yellow belly. Bold white stripes just above and below the eyes. White rump and wing patches flash when in flight.

Female: finely barred black-and-white back with a brown head, yellow belly, no wing patches

Juvenile: similar to female

Nest: cavity; male builds; 1 brood per year

Eggs: 3-7; pale white without markings

Incubation: 12-14 days; male and female incubate

Fledging: 21-28 days; female and male feed young

Migration: complete, to Mexico and Central America

Food: insects, tree sap

Compare: Lewis's Woodpecker (pg. 227) has a red face and belly. Male Williamson's is similar to the Red-naped Sapsucker (pg. 29), which has white on the back and red on the head. Female Williamson's is similar to Northern Flicker (pg. 123), but Flicker has a brown back and gray head.

Stan's Notes: Largest sapsucker species with a striking difference between males and females. Occupies coniferous forests, foraging for insects and drilling sap wells nearly exclusively in conifers. The males drum early in spring to attract mates and to claim territories. Like the other sapsuckers, they have an irregular cadence to their drumming. The males excavate new cavities each year, often in the same tree. Males do more incubating than females.

male

female

HAIRY WOODPECKER
Picoides villosus

YEAR-ROUND

Size: 9" (22.5 cm)

Male: Black-and-white woodpecker with a white belly, and black wings with rows of white spots. White stripe down back. Long black bill. Red mark on back of head.

Female: same as male, but lacks a red mark on head

Juvenile: grayer version of female

Nest: cavity; female and male excavate; 1 brood per year

Eggs: 3-6; white without markings

Incubation: 11-15 days; female and male incubate, the female during day, male at night

Fledging: 28-30 days; male and female feed young

Migration: non-migrator

Food: insects, nuts, seeds; comes to seed and suet feeders

Compare: Larger than Downy Woodpecker (pg. 25), Hairy has a longer bill and lacks Downy's black spots along tail.

Stan's Notes: A common woodpecker of wooded backyards that announces its arrival with a sharp chirp before landing on feeders. This bird is responsible for eating many destructive forest insects. Has a barbed tongue, which helps it extract insects from trees. Tiny bristle-like feathers at the base of bill protect the nostrils from wood dust. Drums on hollow logs, branches or stovepipes in springtime to announce its territory. Often prefers to excavate nest cavities in live aspen trees. Has a larger, more oval-shaped cavity entrance than that of Downy Woodpecker.

BLACK-NECKED STILT
Himantopus mexicanus

SUMMER

Size: 14" (36 cm)

Male: Upper parts of the head, neck and back are black. Lower parts are white. Ridiculously long red-to-pink legs. Long black bill.

Female: similar to male, only browner on back

Juvenile: similar to female, brown instead of black

Nest: ground; the female and male build; 1 brood per year

Eggs: 3-5; off-white with dark markings

Incubation: 22-26 days; female and male incubate, the male during day, female at night

Fledging: 28-32 days; female and male feed young

Migration: complete, to South America

Food: aquatic insects

Compare: Outrageous length of the red-to-pink legs make this shorebird hard to confuse with any other.

Stan's Notes: A summer resident in the southern quarter of Idaho. Also found along the West coast and as far north as the Great Lakes. A bird of shallow freshwater and saltwater marshes, it is very vocal, giving a "kek-kek-kek" call. Legs are up to 10 inches (25 cm) long and may be the longest legs in the bird world in proportion to the body. Nests solitarily or in small colonies in open areas. Known for transporting water with water-soaked belly feathers (belly-soaking) to cool eggs during hot weather. Aggressively defends its nest, eggs and young. Young leave the nest shortly after hatching.

female pg. 135

male

LESSER SCAUP
Aythya affinis

YEAR-ROUND
MIGRATION

Size: 16-17" (40-43 cm)

Male: Appears mostly black with bold white sides and gray back. Chest and head look nearly black, but head appears purple with green highlights in direct sun. Bright yellow eyes.

Female: overall brown with dull white patch at base of light gray bill, yellow eyes

Juvenile: same as female

Nest: ground; female builds; 1 brood per year

Eggs: 8-14; olive buff without markings

Incubation: 22-28 days; female incubates

Fledging: 45-50 days; female teaches young to feed

Migration: complete, to western coastal U.S., southern states, Mexico, Central America, northern South America

Food: aquatic plants and insects

Compare: Larger than American Coot (pg. 15), which lacks male Scaup's white sides. Look for the distinctive white sides of the male Scaup to help identify. The male Blue-winged Teal (pg. 131) is smaller and has a bright white crescent-shaped patch near base of bill.

Stan's Notes: A common diving duck. Often seen in large flocks on lakes, ponds and sewage lagoons. Completely submerges itself to feed on the bottom of lakes (unlike dabbling ducks, which only tip forward to reach bottom). Note the bold white stripe under the wings when in flight. Has an interesting baby-sitting arrangement in which groups of young are tended by one to three adult females.

winter

breeding

AMERICAN AVOCET
Recurvirostra americana

Size: 18" (45 cm)

Male: Black and white back, white belly. A long, thin upturned bill and long gray legs. Head and neck rusty red during breeding, gray in the winter.

Female: similar to male, only with a more strongly upturned bill

Juvenile: similar to adults, with a slight wash of rusty red on neck and head

Nest: ground; the female and male build; 1 brood per year

Eggs: 3-5; light olive with brown markings

Incubation: 22-29 days; female and male incubate

Fledging: 28-35 days; female and male feed young

Migration: complete, to southwestern states, Mexico

Food: insects, crustaceans, aquatic vegetation and fruit

Compare: One of the few long-legged shorebirds in Idaho. Look for the obvious rusty red head of breeding Avocet and long upturned bill.

Stan's Notes: A handsome long-legged bird that prefers shallow alkaline, saline or brackish water, it is well adapted to arid western U.S. conditions. Uses its up-curved bill to sweep from side to side across mud bottoms in search of insects. Both the male and female have a brood patch to incubate eggs and brood their young. Nests in the southern third of Idaho in loose colonies of up to 20 pairs. All members of the colony will defend together against intruders.

male

female

PILEATED WOODPECKER
Dryocopus pileatus

YEAR-ROUND

Size: 19" (48 cm)

Male: Crow-sized woodpecker with a black back and bright red crest. Long gray bill with red mustache. White leading edge of the wings flashes brightly when flying.

Female: same as male, but has a black forehead and lacks red mustache

Juvenile: similar to adults, only duller and browner

Nest: cavity; male and female excavate; 1 brood per year

Eggs: 3-5; white without markings

Incubation: 15-18 days; female and male incubate, the female during day, male at night

Fledging: 26-28 days; female and male feed young

Migration: non-migrator

Food: insects; will come to suet feeders

Compare: This bird is quite distinctive and unlikely to be confused with any others. Look for the Pileated Woodpecker's bright red crest and exceptionally large size.

Stan's Notes: Our largest woodpecker. The common name comes from the Latin *pileatus*, which means "wearing a cap," referring to its crest. Relatively shy bird that prefers large tracts of woodland. Drums on hollow branches, chimneys, etc., to announce territory. Excavates oval holes up to several feet long in tree trunks, looking for insects to eat. Large chips of wood lay at bases of excavated trees. Favorite food is carpenter ants. Young are fed regurgitated insects.

BLACK-BILLED MAGPIE
Pica hudsonia

YEAR-ROUND

Size: 20" (50 cm)

Male: A large black-and-white bird with very long tail and white belly. Iridescent green wings and tail in direct sunlight. Large black bill and legs. White wing patches flash in flight.

Female: same as male

Juvenile: same as adult, but shorter tail

Nest: modified pendulous; the female and male build; 1 brood per year

Eggs: 5-8; green with brown markings

Incubation: 16-21 days; female incubates

Fledging: 25-29 days; female and male feed young

Migration: non-migrator

Food: insects, carrion, fruit, seeds

Compare: Contrasting black-and-white colors and the very long tail of Magpie distinguish it from the all-black American Crow (pg. 17).

Stan's Notes: A wonderfully intelligent bird that is able to mimic dogs, cats and even people. Will often raid a barnyard dog dish for food. Feeds on a variety of food from road kill to insects and seeds it collects from the ground. Easily identified by its bold black-and-white colors and long streaming tail. Travels in small flocks, usually family members, and tends to be very gregarious. Breeds in small colonies with unusual dome nest (dome-shaped roof) deep within thick shrubs. Will mate with same mate for several years. Prefers open fields with cattle or sheep, where it feeds on insects attracted to the livestock.

rushing

weed dance

WESTERN GREBE
Aechmophorus occidentalis

MIGRATION
SUMMER

Size: 24" (60 cm)

Male: A long-necked, nearly all-black water bird with white chin, neck, chest and belly. Long yellow bill and bright red eyes. Dark crown extends around eyes to base of bill. During winter, becomes light gray around eyes.

Female: same as male

Juvenile: similar to adult

Nest: platform; female and male build; 1 brood per year

Eggs: 3-4; bluish white with brown markings

Incubation: 20-23 days; female and male incubate

Fledging: 65-75 days; female and male feed young

Migration: complete, to western coastal U.S.

Food: fish, aquatic insects

Compare: A familiar long-necked water bird. Striking black and white plumage makes it hard to confuse with any other bird.

Stan's Notes: Well known for its unusual breeding dance known as rushing. Side by side, with necks outstretched, mates will spring to their webbed feet and dance across the water's surface (see inset), diving underwater at the end of the rush. Often holds long stalks of water plants in bill when courting mate, called the weed dance (see inset). Its legs are positioned far back on the body, making it difficult to walk on ground. Shortly after choosing a large lake for breeding and till late in summer, it rarely flies. Young ride on backs of adults, climbing on only minutes after hatching. Nests in large colonies of up to 100 pairs on lakes with lots of tall vegetation.

soaring

OSPREY
Pandion haliaetus

SUMMER

Size: 24" (60 cm); up to 5½-foot wingspan

Male: Large eagle-like bird with a white chest and belly, and a nearly black back. White head with a black streak through the eyes. Large wings with black "wrist" marks. Dark bill.

Female: same as male, but larger, with a necklace of brown streaking

Juvenile: similar to adults, with a light tan breast

Nest: platform, often on raised wooden platform; female and male build; 1 brood per year

Eggs: 2-4; white with brown markings

Incubation: 32-42 days; female and male incubate

Fledging: 48-58 days; male and female feed young

Migration: complete, to southern states, Mexico, and Central and South America

Food: fish

Compare: Bald Eagle (pg. 49) is on average 10 inches (25 cm) larger, with an all-white head and tail. The juvenile Bald Eagle is brown with white speckles. Look for a white belly and dark stripe through eyes to identify Osprey.

Stan's Notes: Ospreys are in a family all their own. It is the only raptor that plunges into water feet first to catch fish. Can hover for a few seconds before diving. Carries fish in a head-first position for better aerodynamics. Often harassed by Bald Eagles for its catch. In flight, wings are angled (cocked) backward. Nests on man-made towers and in tall dead trees. Recent studies show male and female might mate for life, but don't migrate to same wintering grounds.

soaring

juvenile

BALD EAGLE
Haliaeetus leucocephalus

YEAR-ROUND

Size: 31-37" (79-94 cm); up to 7-foot wingspan

Male: Pure white head and tail contrast with dark brown-to-black body and wings. A large, curved yellow bill and yellow feet.

Female: same as male, only slightly larger

Juvenile: dark brown with white spots or speckles throughout body and wings, gray bill

Nest: massive platform, usually in a tree; female and male build; 1 brood per year

Eggs: 2; off-white without markings

Incubation: 34-36 days; female and male incubate

Fledging: 75-90 days; female and male feed young

Migration: non-migrator to partial, to southern states

Food: fish, carrion, birds (mainly ducks)

Compare: Golden Eagle (pg. 165) and Turkey Vulture (pg. 21) lack the white head and white tail of adult Bald Eagle. Juvenile Golden Eagle, with its white wrist marks and white base of tail, is similar to the juvenile Bald Eagle.

Stan's Notes: Driven to near extinction due to DDT poisoning and illegal killing. Now making a comeback in North America. Returns to same nest each year, adding more sticks, enlarging it to massive proportions, at times up to 1,000 pounds (450 kg). In the midair mating ritual, one eagle will flip upside down and lock talons with another. Both tumble, then break apart to continue flight. Thought to mate for life, but will switch mates if not successful reproducing. Juvenile attains the white head and tail at about 4 to 5 years of age.

female pg. 79

male

LAZULI BUNTING
Passerina amoena

Size: 5½" (14 cm)

Male: A turquoise blue head, neck, back and tail. Cinnamon chest with cinnamon extending down flanks slightly. White belly. Two bold white wing bars. Non-breeding male has a spotty blue head and back.

Female: overall grayish brown, warm brown breast, a light wash of blue on wings and tail, gray throat, a light gray belly, two narrow white wing bars

Juvenile: similar to adult of the same sex

Nest: cup; female builds; 2-3 broods per year

Eggs: 3-5; pale blue without markings

Incubation: 11-13 days; female incubates

Fledging: 10-12 days; female and male feed young

Migration: complete, to Mexico

Food: insects, seeds

Compare: Smaller than the male Western Bluebird (pg. 57), not as dark blue in color and chest is browner.

Stan's Notes: More common in shrub lands throughout the state. Doesn't like dense forests. Has a strong association with water such as rivers and streams. Gathers in small flocks and tends to move up in elevations after breeding to hunt for insects and search for seeds. It has increased in population and expanded its range over the last 100 years.

SUMMER

TREE SWALLOW
Tachycineta bicolor

Size: 5-6" (13-15 cm)

Male: Blue green in the spring and greener in fall. Appears to change color in direct sunlight. A white belly, a notched tail and pointed wing tips.

Female: similar to male, only duller

Juvenile: gray brown with a white belly and grayish breast band

Nest: cavity; female and male line former woodpecker cavity or nest box; 1 brood per year

Eggs: 4-6; white without markings

Incubation: 13-16 days; female incubates

Fledging: 20-24 days; female and male feed young

Migration: complete, to Mexico and Central America

Food: insects

Compare: Barn Swallow (pg. 55) has a rust belly and deeply forked tail. Similar size as the Cliff Swallow (pg. 81) and Violet-green Swallow (pg. 223), but lacks any tan-to-rust color of the Cliff Swallow and any emerald green of the Violet-green Swallow.

Stan's Notes: The first swallow species to return each spring. Most common along ponds, lakes and agricultural fields. Is attracted to your yard with a nest box. Competes with Western and Mountain Bluebirds for cavities and nest boxes. Travels great distances to find dropped feathers to line its grass nest. Sometimes seen playing, chasing after dropped feathers. Often seen flying back and forth across fields, feeding on insects. Gathers in large flocks to migrate.

BARN SWALLOW
Hirundo rustica

Size: 7" (18 cm)

Male: A sleek swallow with a blue black back, a cinnamon belly and a reddish brown chin. White spots on long forked tail.

Female: same as male, only slightly duller

Juvenile: similar to adults, with a tan belly and chin, and shorter tail

Nest: cup; female and male build; 2 broods a year

Eggs: 4-5; white with brown markings

Incubation: 13-17 days; female incubates

Fledging: 18-23 days; female and male feed young

Migration: complete, to South America

Food: insects, prefers beetles, wasps and flies

Compare: Tree Swallow (pg. 53) has a white belly and chin, and notched tail. Larger than the Cliff Swallow (pg. 81) and Violet-green Swallow (pg. 223), which both lack the distinctive, deeply forked tail. Violet-green Swallow is distinctively green with a white face.

Stan's Notes: Of the seven swallow species in Idaho, this is the only one with a deeply forked tail. Unlike the other swallows, Barn Swallows rarely glide in flight, so look for continuous flapping. It builds a mud nest using up to 1,000 beak-loads of mud, often in or on barns. Nests in colonies of four to six, but nesting alone is not uncommon. Drinks while flying by skimming water or getting water from wet leaves. It also bathes while flying through the rain or sprinklers.

male

female

WESTERN BLUEBIRD
Sialia mexicana

Size: 7" (18 cm)

Male: Deep blue head, neck, back, wings and tail. Rusty red chest and flanks.

Female: similar to male, only duller with gray head

Juvenile: similar to female, with a speckled chest

Nest: cavity, old woodpecker cavity, wooden nest box; female builds; 1-2 broods per year

Eggs: 4-6; pale blue without markings

Incubation: 13-14 days; female incubates

Fledging: 22-23 days; female and male feed young

Migration: complete, southwestern states and Mexico

Food: insects, fruit

Compare: Mountain Bluebird (pg. 59) is similar, but lacks the rusty red breast. Larger than male Lazuli Bunting (pg. 51), which has white wing bars.

Stan's Notes: More common in the Panhandle and northwestern Idaho. It is found in a variety of habitats, from agricultural land to clear-cuts. Wherever it is, it requires a cavity for nesting. Competes with starlings for nest cavities. Like Mountain Bluebirds, Western Bluebirds will use nest boxes, which are responsible for the stable populations. A courting male will fly in front of female, spreading wings and tail, then perch next to her. Often seen going in and out of nest box or cavity as if to say, "Look inside." Male may offer food to female to establish pair bond.

male

female

MOUNTAIN BLUEBIRD
Sialia currucoides

SUMMER

Size: 7" (18 cm)

Male: An overall sky blue bird with a darker blue head, back, wings and tail and white lower belly. Thin black bill.

Female: similar to male, but paler with a nearly gray head and chest and a whitish belly

Juvenile: similar to adult of the same sex

Nest: cavity, old woodpecker cavity, wooden nest box; female builds; 1-2 broods per year

Eggs: 4-6; pale blue without markings

Incubation: 13-14 days; female incubates

Fledging: 22-23 days; female and male feed young

Migration: complete, to Arizona, California, Mexico

Food: insects

Compare: Similar to Western Bluebird (pg. 57), but not as dark blue and lacks Western's rusty red chest.

Stan's Notes: Common in open mountainous country, this bird nests throughout Idaho. Due to conservation of suitable nest sites (dead trees with cavities and man-made nest boxes), populations have increased dramatically over the past 50 years. Like other bluebirds, Mountain Bluebirds take well to nest boxes and tolerate close contact with humans. Young will imprint on their first nest box or cavity, then choose a similar type of box or cavity throughout the rest of life.

Interior

Pacific

YEAR-ROUND

STELLER'S JAY
Cyanocitta stelleri

Size: 11" (28 cm)

Male: Dark blue wings, tail and belly. Black head, nape of the neck and chest. Large, pointed black crest on head that can be lifted at will.

Female: same as male

Juvenile: similar to adult

Nest: cup; female and male build; 1 brood a year

Eggs: 3-5; pale green with brown markings

Incubation: 14-16 days; female incubates

Fledging: 16-18 days; female and male feed young

Migration: non-migrator

Food: insects, berries, seeds; will visit seed feeders

Compare: Gray Jay (pg. 199) lacks any blue coloring and a crest.

Stan's Notes: A common resident of coniferous forests below the timberline. Often found in suburban yards. It rarely competes with Gray Jays, which occupy higher elevations. Thought to mate for life, rarely dispersing far, usually breeding within 10 miles (16 km) of the place of birth. Several subspecies are seen throughout the West, with two forms in Idaho. The Interior variety has a black crest with distinct white streaks and the Pacific has a solid black crest.

male

female

BELTED KINGFISHER
Ceryle alcyon

YEAR-ROUND

Size: 13" (33 cm)

Male: Large blue bird with white belly. Broad blue gray breast band and a ragged crest that is raised and lowered at will. Large head with a long, thick black bill. A small white spot directly in front of red brown eyes. Black wing tips with splashes of white that flash when flying.

Female: same as male, but with rusty breast band in addition to blue gray band, and rusty flanks

Juvenile: similar to female

Nest: cavity; female and male excavate; 1 brood per year

Eggs: 6-7; white without markings

Incubation: 23-24 days; female and male incubate

Fledging: 23-24 days; female and male feed young

Migration: non-migrator in Idaho

Food: small fish

Compare: Kingfisher is rarely found away from water.

Stan's Notes: Seen perched on branches near the water, it dives headfirst for small fish and returns to a branch to eat. Has a loud machine-gun-like call. Excavates a deep cavity in bank of river or lake. Parents drop dead fish into water, teaching the young to dive. Regurgitates pellets of bone after meals, being unable to pass bones through digestive tract. Mates recognize each other by call.

CHESTNUT-BACKED CHICKADEE
Poecile rufescens

YEAR-ROUND

Size: 4¾" (12 cm)

Male: Rich, warm chestnut back and sides. Black crown and chin. White cheeks and sides of head. Gray wings and tail.

Female: same as male

Juvenile: same as adult

Nest: cavity; female and male build; 1-2 broods per year

Eggs: 5-7; white without markings

Incubation: 10-12 days; female incubates

Fledging: 13-16 days; female and male feed young

Migration: non-migrator

Food: insects, seeds, fruit; comes to seed and suet feeders

Compare: The Black-capped Chickadee (pg. 175) and Mountain Chickadee (pg. 177) are similar, but both lack Chestnut-backed's distinctive chestnut-colored back.

Stan's Notes: The most colorful of all chickadees. Like the other chickadee species, the Chestnut-backed clings to branches upside down, looking for insects. During breeding, it is quiet and secretive. In winter it joins other birds such as kinglets, nuthatches and other chickadees. It prefers humid coniferous forests with hemlock and Tamarack. Uses a cavity nest from 2 to 20 feet (up to 6 m) off the ground. Will use the same nest year after year. Comes to seed and suet feeders.

BROWN CREEPER
Certhia americana

Size: 5" (13 cm)

Male: Small, thin, nearly camouflaged brown bird. White from chin to belly. White eyebrows. Long stiff tail. Dark eyes. Thin curved bill.

Female: same as male

Juvenile: same as adult

Nest: cup; female builds; unknown how many broods per year

Eggs: 5-6; white with tiny brown markings

Incubation: 14-17 days; female incubates, male feeds female during incubation

Fledging: 13-16 days; female and male feed young

Migration: partial migrator to non-migrator

Food: insects, nuts, seeds

Compare: Creeps up tree trunks, not down, like the White-breasted Nuthatch (pg. 181). Watch for Creeper to fly from the top of one trunk to the bottom of another, working its way to the top, looking for insects. Slightly larger than the Red-breasted Nuthatch (pg. 173), with a similar white stripe above eyes, but Creeper has a white belly, long tail and lacks a black crown.

Stan's Notes: This bird utilizes its camouflage coloring to defend itself, spreading out flat on a branch or tree trunk without moving. Young are able to follow their parents, creeping soon after fledging. Commonly found in wooded areas. Often builds nest behind loose bark of dead or dying trees.

SUMMER

CHIPPING SPARROW
Spizella passerina

Size: 5" (13 cm)

Male: Small gray brown sparrow with a clear gray chest, rusty crown, white eyebrows with a black eye line, thin gray black bill and two faint wing bars.

Female: same as male

Juvenile: similar to adult, has a streaked breast, lacks the rusty crown

Nest: cup; female builds; 2 broods per year

Eggs: 3-5; blue green with brown markings

Incubation: 11-14 days; female incubates

Fledging: 10-12 days; female and male feed young

Migration: complete, to southern states, Mexico and Central America

Food: insects, seeds; will come to ground feeders

Compare: The Lark Sparrow (pg. 95) is larger and has a white chest and central spot. Fox Sparrow (pg. 99) is larger and lacks the rusty crown. Smaller than Song Sparrow (pg. 83), which has a heavily streaked chest. Female House Finch (pg. 73) also has a streaked chest.

Stan's Notes: A common garden or yard bird, often seen feeding on dropped seeds below feeders. Gathers in large family groups in autumn to feed in preparation for migration. Migrates during the night in flocks of 20 to 30 birds. Received its common name from the male's slow "chip" call. Often just called Chippy. Nest is placed low in dense shrubs and is almost always lined with animal hair.

PINE SISKIN
Carduelis pinus

YEAR-ROUND

Size: 5" (13 cm)

Male: Small brown finch. Heavily streaked back, breast and belly. Yellow wing bars. Yellow at base of tail. Thin bill.

Female: same as male

Juvenile: similar to adult, light yellow tinge over the breast and chin

Nest: modified cup; the female builds; 2 broods per year

Eggs: 3-4; greenish blue with brown markings

Incubation: 12-13 days; female incubates

Fledging: 14-15 days; female and male feed young

Migration: irruptive; moves around the state in search of food

Food: seeds, insects; will come to seed feeders

Compare: Female American Goldfinch (pg. 265) lacks streaks and has white wing bars. Female House Finch (pg. 73) has a streaked chest, but lacks yellow wing bars.

Stan's Notes: A nesting resident, it is usually considered a winter finch because it is more visible in the non-nesting season, when it gathers in flocks, moves around Idaho and visits feeders. Will come to thistle feeders. Travels and breeds in small groups. Male feeds the female during incubation. Juveniles lose yellow tint by late summer of the first year. Builds its nest toward ends of coniferous branches, where needles are dense, helping to conceal. Nests are often only a few feet apart.

male pg. 245

female

HOUSE FINCH
Carpodacus mexicanus

YEAR-ROUND

Size: 5" (13 cm)

Female: A plain brown bird with a heavily streaked white chest.

Male: orange red face, chest and rump, a brown cap, brown marking behind eyes, brown wings streaked with white, streaked belly

Juvenile: similar to female

Nest: cup, sometimes in cavities; female builds; 2 broods per year

Eggs: 4-5; pale blue, lightly marked

Incubation: 12-14 days; female incubates

Fledging: 15-19 days; female and male feed young

Migration: non-migrator to partial migrator; will move around to find food

Food: seeds, fruit, leaf buds; will visit seed feeders

Compare: Female Cassin's Finch (pg. 91) has a more heavily streaked belly. Similar to Pine Siskin (pg. 71), but lacks yellow wing bars and has a larger bill. Female Goldfinch (pg. 265) has a clear chest and white wing bars.

Stan's Notes: Very social bird. Visits feeders in small flocks. Likes nesting in hanging flower baskets. Incubating female is fed by the male. Has a loud, cheerful warbling song. Historically it occurred from the Pacific coast to the Rockies, with only a few reaching the eastern side. House Finches that were originally introduced to Long Island, New York, from the western U.S. in the 1940s have since populated the entire eastern U.S. Now found all over the country. Suffers from a fatal eye disease that causes eyes to crust over.

SUMMER

HOUSE WREN
Troglodytes aedon

Size: 5" (13 cm)

Male: A small all-brown bird with lighter brown markings on tail and wings. Slightly curved brown bill. Often holds its tail erect.

Female: same as male

Juvenile: same as adult

Nest: cavity; female and male line just about any nest cavity; 2 broods per year

Eggs: 4-6; tan with brown markings

Incubation: 10-13 days; female and male incubate

Fledging: 12-15 days; female and male feed young

Migration: complete, to southern states and Mexico

Food: insects

Compare: Rock Wren (pg. 87) is slightly larger, with fine white speckles on the back, and a light tan belly and breast. House Wren's lack of eyebrows distinguishes it from other wrens. Its long curved bill and long upturned tail differentiates it from sparrows.

Stan's Notes: A prolific songster, it will sing from dawn until dusk during the mating season. Easily attracted to nest boxes. In spring, the male chooses several prospective nesting cavities and places a few small twigs in each. Female inspects each, chooses one, and finishes the nest building. She will completely fill the nest cavity with uniformly small twigs, then line a small depression at back of cavity with pine needles and grass. Often has trouble fitting long twigs through nest cavity hole. Tries many different directions and approaches until successful.

male pg. 179

female

Oregon female

DARK-EYED JUNCO
Junco hyemalis

YEAR-ROUND

Size: 5½" (14 cm)

Female: A round, dark-eyed bird with tan-to-brown chest, head and back. White belly. Ivory-to-pink bill. Since the outermost tail feathers are white, tail appears as a white V in flight.

Male: same as female, only slate gray to charcoal

Juvenile: similar to female, but has a streaked breast and head

Nest: cup; female and male build; 2 broods a year

Eggs: 3-5; white with reddish brown markings

Incubation: 12-13 days; female incubates

Fledging: 10-13 days; male and female feed young

Migration: partial migrator to complete, across the U.S.

Food: seeds, insects; will come to seed feeders

Compare: Rarely confused with any other bird. Small flocks feed under bird feeders in winter.

Stan's Notes: Several junco species have now been combined into one, simply called Dark-eyed Junco (see lower inset). A common year-round resident. One of the most numerous wintering birds in the state, spending winters in foothills and plains after snowmelt, returning to higher elevations for nesting. Nests in a wide variety of wooded habitats in April and May. Usually is seen on the ground in small flocks. It adheres to a rigid social hierarchy, with dominant birds chasing the less dominant birds. Look for its white outer tail feathers flashing in flight. Most comfortable on the ground, juncos will "double-scratch" with both feet to expose seeds and insects. Consumes many weed seeds.

male pg. 51

female

LAZULI BUNTING
Passerina amoena

SUMMER

Size: 5½" (14 cm)

Female: Overall grayish brown with a warm brown chest, light wash of blue on wings and tail, gray throat and light gray belly. Two narrow white wing bars.

Male: turquoise blue head, neck, back and tail, cinnamon chest, white belly and two bold white wing bars

Juvenile: similar to adult of the same sex

Nest: cup; female builds; 2-3 broods per year

Eggs: 3-5; pale blue without markings

Incubation: 11-13 days; female incubates

Fledging: 10-12 days; female and male feed young

Migration: complete, to Mexico

Food: insects, seeds

Compare: The female Western Bluebird (pg. 57) and Mountain Bluebird (pg. 59) are larger, with both showing much more blue than the female Bunting.

Stan's Notes: More common in shrub lands throughout the state. Doesn't like dense forests. Has a strong association with water such as rivers and streams. Gathers in small flocks and tends to move up in elevations after breeding to hunt for insects and search for seeds. It has increased in population and expanded its range over the last 100 years.

SUMMER

CLIFF SWALLOW
Petrochelidon pyrrhonota

Size: 5½" (14 cm)

Male: A uniquely patterned swallow with a dark back, wings and cap. Distinctive tan-to-rust rump, cheeks and forehead.

Female: same as male

Juvenile: similar to adult, lacks distinct patterning

Nest: gourd-shaped, made of mud; the male and female build; 1-2 broods per year

Eggs: 3-6; pale white with brown markings

Incubation: 14-16 days; male and female incubate

Fledging: 21-24 days; female and male feed young

Migration: complete, to South America

Food: insects

Compare: Smaller than Barn Swallow (pg. 55), which has a deeply forked tail and blue back and wings. The Tree Swallow (pg. 53) lacks any tan-to-rust coloring. Violet-green Swallow (pg. 223) is green with a bright white face.

Stan's Notes: A common and widespread swallow species in Idaho during summer. Common around bridges (especially bridges over water) and rural housing (especially in open country close to cliffs). Constructs a gourd-shaped nest with a funnel-like entrance pointing down. A colony nester, with many nests lined up beneath eaves of buildings or under cliff overhangs. Will carry balls of mud up to a mile to construct its nest. Many of the colony return to same nest sites each year. Not unusual for it to have two broods per season. If the number of nests beneath eaves becomes a problem, wait until after young have left the nests to hose off the mud.

YEAR-ROUND

SONG SPARROW
Melospiza melodia

Size: 5-6" (13-15 cm)

Male: Common brown sparrow with heavy dark streaks on breast coalescing into a central dark spot.

Female: same as male

Juvenile: similar to adult, finely streaked breast, lacks a central spot

Nest: cup; female builds; 2 broods per year

Eggs: 3-4; pale blue to green with reddish brown markings

Incubation: 12-14 days; female incubates

Fledging: 9-12 days; female and male feed young

Migration: complete, to southern states, non-migrator in most parts of Idaho

Food: insects, seeds; rarely visits seed feeders

Compare: Similar to other brown sparrows. Look for a heavily streaked chest with central dark spot.

Stan's Notes: Many Song Sparrow subspecies or varieties, but dark central spot carries through each variant. While the female builds another nest for a second brood, the male sparrow often takes over feeding the young. Returns to a similar area each year, defending a small territory by singing from thick shrubs. A common host of the Brown-headed Cowbird. Ground feeders, look for them to scratch simultaneously with both feet to expose seeds. Unlike many other sparrow species, Song Sparrows rarely flock together.

male

female

YEAR-ROUND

HOUSE SPARROW
Passer domesticus

Size: 6" (15 cm)

Male: Medium sparrow-like bird with large black spot on throat extending down to the chest. Brown back and single white wing bars. A gray belly and crown.

Female: all-light-brown bird, slightly smaller, lacks the black throat patch and single wing bars

Juvenile: similar to female

Nest: domed cup nest, within cavity; female and male build; 2-3 broods per year

Eggs: 4-6; white with brown markings

Incubation: 10-12 days; female incubates

Fledging: 14-17 days; female and male feed young

Migration: non-migrator; moves around to find food

Food: seeds, insects, fruit; comes to seed feeders

Compare: The Chipping Sparrow (pg. 69) has a rusty crown. Look for the male House Sparrow's black bib. Female has a clear breast and no marking on head (cap).

Stan's Notes: One of the first bird songs heard in cities in spring. Familiar city bird, nearly always in flocks. Introduced from Europe to Central Park, New York, in 1850 and now found throughout North America. These birds are not really sparrows, but members of the Weaver Finch family, characterized by their large, oversized domed nests. Constructs a nest containing scraps of plastic, paper and whatever else is available. An aggressive bird that will kill the young of other birds in order to take over a cavity.

ROCK WREN
Salpinctes obsoletus

YEAR-ROUND
SUMMER

Size: 6" (15 cm)

Male: Overall grayish brown with tinges of buffy brown on tail and wings. Gray back, often finely speckled with white. Belly and breast are light tan.

Female: same as male

Juvenile: similar to adult

Nest: crevice; male and female build; 1-2 broods per year

Eggs: 4-8; white with light brown markings

Incubation: 14-16 days; female and male incubate

Fledging: 14-18 days; female and male feed young

Migration: complete, to southern states

Food: insects

Compare: Slightly larger than House Wren (pg. 75), which lacks the Rock Wren's white speckles on back.

Stan's Notes: Consistently uses open sunny piles of broken rocks (scree) and rock debris at cliff bases (talus slopes) for nesting. Often builds a small runway of flat stones leading up to the nest, which is usually in a rock crevice. Known to also nest on prairies, where it uses dirt banks instead of rock piles. Begins nesting in May, with the female doing most of the incubating and the male feeding the female during incubation.

male

female

GRAY-CROWNED ROSY-FINCH
Leucosticte tephrocotis

YEAR-ROUND
WINTER

Size: 6" (15 cm)

Male: Gray crown with a black forehead, chin and throat. Warm cinnamon-brown body with a wash of rosy red, especially along flanks and rump.

Female: same as male, but has less pink

Juvenile: similar to adult of the same sex

Nest: cup; female builds; 1-2 broods per year

Eggs: 3-5; white without markings

Incubation: 12-14 days; female incubates

Fledging: 16-18 days; female and male feed young

Migration: complete, to higher elevations of western states

Food: seeds, insects; will visit seed feeders

Compare: Similar to other rosy-finches, but the Gray-crowned has a black forehead, throat and chin. The female Cassin's Finch (pg. 91) and female House Finch (pg. 73) lack the characteristic gray crown of Gray-crowned Rosy-Finch.

Stan's Notes: Found in high alpine regions, nesting in steep cliff faces. Year-round resident, but breeding birds in Canada and Alaska move into the state during winter, swelling the population. Almost always seen in small flocks, foraging on the ground near patches of snow. During breeding, both male and female develop an opening in the floor of mouth (buccal pouch), which is used for carrying a large supply of food, such as insects, to the young in the nest.

female

male pg. 247

CASSIN'S FINCH
Carpodacus cassinii

YEAR-ROUND
SUMMER

Size: 6½" (16 cm)

Female: Brown-to-gray finch with fine black streaks on back and wings. Heavily streaked white chest and belly.

Male: light wash of crimson red, especially bright red crown, brown streaks on the back and wings, white belly

Juvenile: similar to female

Nest: cup; female builds; 1-2 broods per year

Eggs: 3-5; white without markings

Incubation: 12-14 days; female incubates

Fledging: 14-18 days; female and male feed young

Migration: partial migrator to non-migrator; will move around to find food

Food: seeds, insects, fruits, berries; will visit seed feeders

Compare: The female House Finch (pg. 73) is similar, but has a gray belly that is not as streaked. Lacks the characteristic gray head markings of the Gray-crowned Rosy-Finch (pg. 89).

Stan's Notes: A common mountain finch of coniferous forests. It usually forages for seeds on the ground, but eats evergreen buds and aspen and willow catkins. Breeds in May. A colony nester, depending on the regional food source. The more food available, the larger the colony. Male sings a rapid warble, often imitating other birds such as jays, tanagers and grosbeaks. A cowbird host.

female

male pg. 27

non-breeding male

SUMMER

LARK BUNTING
Calamospiza melanocorys

Size: 6½" (16 cm)

Female: Brown bird with heavily streaked chest and a white belly. Black vertical line on each side of white chin. May have a central dark spot on the chest. Faint white eyebrows.

Male: black bird with a large broad head, white wing patches and large bluish gray bill

Juvenile: similar to adult of the same sex

Nest: cup; female builds; 1-2 broods per year

Eggs: 4-6; pale blue with markings

Incubation: 11-13 days; female and male incubate

Fledging: 8-12 days; female and male feed young

Migration: complete, to southwestern states, Mexico

Food: insects, seeds

Compare: Appears similar to open country sparrows. The female Red-winged Blackbird (pg. 111) lacks the white belly and chin.

Stan's Notes: Common in eastern and southern parts of Idaho in dry plains and sagebrush regions. Has short rounded wings. Flying with shallow wing beats, the male flashes white wing patches. Male takes to air to display to female, setting its wings in a V position and floating back, rocking like a butterfly, singing a most amazing song. Song is like the song of Old World larks, hence the common name. Will flock with hundreds, if not thousands, of other Lark Buntings in autumn for migration.

MIGRATION
SUMMER

LARK SPARROW
Chondestes grammacus

Size: 6½" (16 cm)

Male: All-brown bird with unique rust red, white and black head pattern. White breast with a central black spot. Gray rump and white edges to gray tail, as seen in flight.

Female: same as male

Juvenile: similar to adult, no rust red on head

Nest: cup, on the ground; female builds; 1 brood per year

Eggs: 3-6; pale white with brown markings

Incubation: 10-12 days; male and female incubate

Fledging: 10-12 days; female and male feed young

Migration: complete, coastal Mexico, Central America

Food: seeds, insects

Compare: White-crowned Sparrow (pg. 97) lacks the Lark Sparrow's rust red pattern on the head and central spot on a white breast. Larger than the Chipping Sparrow (pg. 69), which has a similar rusty color on head, but lacks Lark's white breast and central spot.

Stan's Notes: One of the larger sparrow species and one of the best songsters, also well known for its courtship strutting, chasing and lark-like flight pattern (rapid wing beats with tail spread). A bird of open fields, pastures and prairies, found almost anywhere there are no mountains. Very common during migration, when large flocks congregate. Uses nest for several years if first brood is successful.

juvenile

WHITE-CROWNED SPARROW
Zonotrichia leucophrys

YEAR-ROUND
SUMMER

Size: 6½-7½" (16-19 cm)

Male: A brown sparrow with a gray breast and a black-and-white striped crown. Small, thin pink bill.

Female: same as male

Juvenile: similar to adult, with brown stripes on the head instead of white

Nest: cup; female builds; 2 broods per year

Eggs: 3-5; color varies from greenish to bluish to whitish with red brown markings

Incubation: 11-14 days; female incubates

Fledging: 8-12 days; male and female feed young

Migration: complete, to Pacific coast, southern states and Mexico, non-migrator in parts of Idaho

Food: insects, seeds, berries; visits ground feeders

Compare: Lark Sparrow (pg. 95) has a rust red pattern on the head and a central black spot on a white breast.

Stan's Notes: Year-round resident in parts of Idaho. Usually seen in groups of up to 20 during migration, when it can be seen feeding beneath seed feeders. Feeds on the ground, scratching backward with both feet simultaneously. Males arrive before the females and establish territories by singing from perches. Nesting begins in May. Male assumes most of the responsibility of raising the young while female starts the second brood. Only 9 to 12 days separate broods.

SUMMER

FOX SPARROW
Passerella iliaca

Size: 7" (18 cm)

Male: Plump brown sparrow with a gray head, back and rump. White chest and belly with rusty brown streaks. Rusty tail and wings.

Female: same as male

Juvenile: same as adult

Nest: cup; female builds; 2 broods per year

Eggs: 2-4; pale green with reddish markings

Incubation: 12-14 days; female incubates

Fledging: 10-11 days; female and male feed young

Migration: complete, to western coastal U.S., southern states

Food: seeds, insects; comes to feeders

Compare: Male and female Spotted Towhee (pg. 7) are found in a similar habitat, but the male has a black head and both have white bellies without streaking.

Stan's Notes: One of the largest sparrows. Several color variations of Fox Sparrow, depending upon the part of the country. In Idaho, identifying them is more difficult because some have gray heads, while others have red heads. Builds nest in brush on the ground and along forest edges. Scratches like a chicken with both feet at the same time to find seeds and insects. "Sparrow" comes from the Anglo-Saxon word *spearwa*, meaning "flutterer," as applies to any small bird. "Fox" refers to the bird's rusty color.

HORNED LARK
Eremophila alpestris

Size: 7-8" (18-20 cm)

Male: Brown with a slightly orange nape of neck. Black necklace. Yellow chin and forehead. Black spot near eyes, behind black bill. Two tiny "horns" on head can be hard to see.

Female: same as male, only duller, "horns" are even less noticeable

Juvenile: lacks the black markings and yellow chin, doesn't form "horns" until second year

Nest: ground; female builds; 2-3 broods per year

Eggs: 3-4; gray with brown markings

Incubation: 11-12 days; female incubates

Fledging: 9-12 days; female and male feed young

Migration: non-migrator to partial migrator in Idaho

Food: seeds, insects

Compare: Smaller than Meadowlark (pg. 283), which shares the black necklace and yellow chin. Look for the black marks in front of eyes.

Stan's Notes: The only true lark native to North America. A year-round resident, but also moves to find food (seasonal movement). Larks are birds of open ground. Common in rural areas, almost always seen in large flocks at country roads. Population increased over the past 100 years due to clearing land for farming. May have up to three broods per year because they get such an early start. Females perform a fluttering distraction display if nest is disturbed. Females can renest about seven days after brood fledges. The name "Lark" comes from the Middle English word *laverock*, or "a lark."

1 year old

CEDAR WAXWING
Bombycilla cedrorum

Size: 7½" (19 cm)

Male: Very sleek-looking gray-to-brown bird with pointed crest, light yellow belly and bandit-like black mask. Tip of tail is bright yellow and the tips of wings look as if they have been dipped in red wax.

Female: same as male

Juvenile: grayish with a heavily streaked chest, lacks red wing tips, black mask and sleek look

Nest: cup; female and male build; 1 brood a year, occasionally 2

Eggs: 4-6; pale blue with brown markings

Incubation: 10-12 days; female incubates

Fledging: 14-18 days; female and male feed young

Migration: partial migrator; moves around to find food

Food: cedar cones, fruit, insects

Compare: Nearly identical to its larger, less common cousin, Bohemian Waxwing (not shown).

Stan's Notes: The name is derived from its red wax-like wing tips and preference for eating small blueberry-like cones of the cedar. Mostly seen in flocks, moving from area to area, looking for berries. Wanders in winter to find available food supplies. Seen more often in winter because naked branches reveal its presence. In summer, before berries are abundant, it feeds on insects. Spends most of its time at the tops of tall trees. Listen for the very high-pitched "sreee" whistling sounds it constantly makes. Obtains mask after first year and red wing tips after second year.

male pg. 3

female

SUMMER

BLACK-HEADED GROSBEAK
Pheucticus melanocephalus

Size: 8" (20 cm)

Female: Appears like an overgrown sparrow. Overall brown with lighter-colored chest and belly, prominent white eyebrows and a large two-toned bill.

Male: burnt orange chest, neck and rump, black head, tail and wings with irregular-shaped white wing patches, large bill with upper bill darker than lower

Juvenile: similar to adult of the same sex

Nest: cup; female builds; 1 brood per year

Eggs: 3-4; pale green or bluish, brown markings

Incubation: 11-13 days; female and male incubate

Fledging: 11-13 days; female and male feed young

Migration: complete, to Mexico, Central America and South America

Food: insects, seeds, fruit

Compare: Female House Finch (pg. 73) is smaller, has more streaking on the chest and bill isn't as large. Look for female Grosbeak's unusual bicolored bill.

Stan's Notes: A cosmopolitan bird that nests in a wide variety of habitats, seeming to prefer the foothills slightly more than other places. Both males and females sing and aggressively defend their nests against intruders. Song is very similar to the American Robin's and Western Tanager's, making it hard to tell them apart by song. Populations are increasing in Idaho and across the U.S.

female

male pg. 9

RED-WINGED BLACKBIRD
Agelaius phoeniceus

Size: 8½" (22 cm)

Female: Heavily streaked brown bird with a pointed brown bill and white eyebrows.

Male: jet black bird with red and yellow patches on upper wings, pointed black bill

Juvenile: same as female

Nest: cup; female builds; 2-3 broods per year

Eggs: 3-4; bluish green with brown markings

Incubation: 10-12 days; female incubates

Fledging: 11-14 days; female and male feed young

Migration: partial migrator to non-migrator; will move around the state to find food in winter

Food: seeds, insects; will come to seed feeders

Compare: Female Brewer's Blackbird (pg. 113) and female Yellow-headed Blackbird (pg. 117) are larger. Female Brown-headed Cowbird (pg. 105) is smaller. All three species lack white eyebrows and heavily streaked chest of the female Red-winged Blackbird.

Stan's Notes: One of the most widespread and numerous birds in Idaho. It is a sure sign of spring when the Red-winged Blackbirds return to the marshes. Flocks of up to 100,000 birds have been reported. Males return before the females and defend territories by singing from tops of surrounding vegetation. Males repeat call from the tops of cattails while showing off their red and yellow wing bars (epaulets). Females choose mate and usually will nest over shallow water in thick stands of cattails. Red-wingeds feed mostly on seeds in fall and spring, switching to insects during summer.

111

male pg. 11

female

BREWER'S BLACKBIRD
Euphagus cyanocephalus

YEAR-ROUND
SUMMER

Size: 9" (22.5 cm)

Female: An overall grayish brown bird. Legs and bill nearly black. While most have dark eyes, some have bright white or pale yellow eyes.

Male: glossy black, shining green in direct light, head purplish, white or pale yellow eyes

Juvenile: similar to female

Nest: cup; female builds; 1-2 broods per year

Eggs: 4-6; gray with brown markings

Incubation: 12-14 days; female incubates

Fledging: 13-14 days; female and male feed young

Migration: non-migrator to partial migrator in Idaho

Food: insects, seeds, fruit

Compare: Larger in size and darker in color than the female Brown-headed Cowbird (pg. 105). Female Red-winged Blackbird (pg. 111) is similar in size, but has a heavily streaked chest and prominent white eyebrows.

Stan's Notes: Common blackbird often found in association with agricultural lands and seen in open areas such as wet pastures and mountain meadows up to 10,000 feet (3,050 m). Male and some females are easily identified by their bright, nearly white eyes. It will usually nest in a shrub, small tree or directly on the ground. Prefers to nest in small colonies of up to 20 pairs. Will flock with other blackbird family members such as Red-wingeds and cowbirds. A common cowbird host. Gathers in large flocks for fall migration. It is expanding its range in North America.

in flight

COMMON NIGHTHAWK
Chordeiles minor

SUMMER

Size: 9" (22.5 cm)

Male: A camouflaged brown and white bird with white chin. A distinctive white band across wings and the tail, seen only in flight.

Female: similar to male, but with tan chin, lacks the white tail band

Juvenile: similar to female

Nest: no nest; lays eggs on the ground, usually on rocks, or on rooftop; 1 brood per year

Eggs: 2; cream with lavender markings

Incubation: 19-20 days; female and male incubate

Fledging: 20-21 days; female and male feed young

Migration: complete, to South America

Food: insects caught in air

Compare: Look for the obvious white wing band of Nighthawk in flight, and the characteristic flap-flap-flap-glide flight pattern.

Stan's Notes: Usually only seen flying at dusk or after sunset, but not uncommon for it to be sitting on a fence post, sleeping during the day. A very noisy bird, repeating a "peenting" call during flight. Alternates slow wing beats with bursts of quick wing beats. Prolific insect eater. Prefers gravel rooftops for nesting in cities and nests on the ground in country. Male's distinctive springtime mating ritual is a steep diving flight terminated with a loud popping noise. One of the first birds to migrate each fall, starting in August.

115

male pg. 13

female

YELLOW-HEADED BLACKBIRD
Xanthocephalus xanthocephalus

Size: 9-11" (22.5-28 cm)

Female: A large brown bird with a dull yellow head and chest. Slightly smaller than male.

Male: black bird with a lemon yellow head, chest and nape of neck, black mask and gray bill, white wing patches

Juvenile: similar to female

Nest: cup; female builds; 2 broods per year

Eggs: 3-5; greenish white with brown markings

Incubation: 11-13 days; female incubates

Fledging: 9-12 days; female feeds young

Migration: complete, to southern states and Mexico

Food: insects, seeds

Compare: Larger than female Red-winged Blackbird (pg. 111), which has white eyebrows and streaked chest.

Stan's Notes: Usually heard before seen, Yellow-headed Blackbird has a low, hoarse, raspy or metallic call. Nests in deep water marshes unlike its cousin, the Red-winged Blackbird, which prefers shallow water. The male gives an impressive mating display, flying with head drooped and feet and tail pointing down while steadily beating its wings. The female incubates alone and feeds between three to five young. Young keep low and out of sight for up to three weeks before starting to fly. Migrates in flocks of up to 200 with other blackbirds. Flocks made up mainly of males return first in early April; females return later. Most colonies consist of 20 to 100 nests.

KILLDEER
Charadrius vociferus

YEAR-ROUND
SUMMER

Size: 11" (28 cm)

Male: An upland shorebird with two black bands around the neck like a necklace. A brown back and white belly. Bright reddish orange rump, visible in flight.

Female: same as male

Juvenile: similar to adult, with only one neck band

Nest: ground; male builds; 2 broods per year

Eggs: 3-5; tan with brown markings

Incubation: 24-28 days; male and female incubate

Fledging: 25 days; male and female lead their young to food

Migration: complete, southern states, Mexico, Central America, non-migrator in most of Idaho

Food: insects

Compare: The Spotted Sandpiper (pg. 107) is found around water and lacks the two neck bands of the Killdeer.

Stan's Notes: The only shorebird with two black neck bands. It is known for its broken wing impression, which draws intruders away from nest. Once clear of the nest, the Killdeer takes flight. Nests are only a slight depression in a gravel area, often very difficult to see. Young look like yellow cotton balls on stilts when first hatched, but quickly molt to appear similar to parents. Able to follow parents and peck for insects soon after birth. Is technically classified as a shorebird, but doesn't live at the shore. Often found in vacant fields or along railroads. Has a very distinctive "kill-jer" call.

male

female

AMERICAN KESTREL
Falco sparverius

Size: 10-12" (25-30 cm); up to 2-foot wingspan

Male: Rusty brown back and tail. A white breast with dark spots. Double black vertical lines on white face. Blue gray wings. Distinctive wide black band with a white edge on tip of rusty tail.

Female: similar to male, but slightly larger, has rusty brown wings and dark bands on tail

Juvenile: same as adult of the same sex

Nest: cavity; doesn't build a nest within; 1 brood per year

Eggs: 4-5; white with brown markings

Incubation: 29-31 days; male and female incubate

Fledging: 30-31 days; female and male feed young

Migration: non-migrator to partial migrator in Idaho

Food: insects, small mammals and birds, reptiles

Compare: Similar to other falcons. Look for the two vertical black stripes on face of Kestrel. No other small bird of prey has rusty-colored back or tail.

Stan's Notes: Formerly called Sparrow Hawk due to its small size. Could be called Grasshopper Hawk because it eats many grasshoppers. Hovers near roads before diving for prey. Adapts quickly to a wooden nesting box. Has pointed swept-back wings, seen in flight. Perches nearly upright. Unusual raptor in that males and females have quite different markings. Watch for them to pump their tails up and down after landing on perches.

red-shafted
male

yellow-shafted
female

yellow-shafted
male

red-shafted
female

NORTHERN FLICKER
Colaptes auratus

YEAR-ROUND

Size: 12" (30 cm)

Male: Brown and black woodpecker with a large white rump patch visible only when flying. Black necklace above a speckled chest. Gray head with a brown cap. Red mustache.

Female: same as male, but lacking a red mustache

Juvenile: same as adult of the same sex

Nest: cavity; female and male excavate; 1 brood per year

Eggs: 5-8; white without markings

Incubation: 11-14 days; female and male incubate

Fledging: 25-28 days; female and male feed young

Migration: non-migrator in Idaho

Food: insects, especially ants and beetles

Compare: Female Williamson's Sapsucker (pg. 31) has a finely barred back with a yellow belly and lacks Flicker's black spots on chest and belly.

Stan's Notes: The flicker is the only woodpecker to regularly feed on the ground, preferring ants and beetles. Produces antacid saliva to neutralize the acidic defense of ants. Male usually selects a nest site, taking up to 12 days to excavate. Some have been successful attracting flickers to nesting boxes stuffed with sawdust. Northern Flickers in western states flash reddish orange under the wings and tails when flying, while those in eastern states have golden yellow wing linings and tails. Both varieties undulate deeply during flight while giving a loud "wacka-wacka" call. Hybrids between western red-shafted and eastern yellow-shafted versions occur in the Great Plains, where their ranges overlap.

MOURNING DOVE
Zenaida macroura

Size: 12" (30 cm)

Male: Smooth fawn-colored dove with gray patch on the head. Iridescent pink, green around neck. A single black spot behind and below eyes. Black spots on wings and tail. Pointed wedge-shaped tail with white edges.

Female: similar to male, lacking iridescent pink and green neck feathers

Juvenile: spotted and streaked

Nest: platform; female and male build; 2 broods per year

Eggs: 2; white without markings

Incubation: 13-14 days; male and female incubate, the male during day, female at night

Fledging: 12-14 days; female and male feed young

Migration: partial to complete, to southern states; will move around to find food

Food: seeds; will visit seed and ground feeders

Compare: Smaller than Rock Dove (pg. 205), lacking its wide range of color combinations.

Stan's Notes: Name comes from its mournful cooing. Mates for life, roughly seven to ten years. A ground feeder, its head bobs as it walks. One of the few birds to drink without lifting head, same as Rock Dove. Parents feed the young a regurgitated liquid called crop-milk for the first few days of life. Flimsy platform nest of twigs often falls apart in a storm. Wind rushing through wing feathers in flight creates a characteristic whistling sound.

PIED-BILLED GREBE
Podilymbus podiceps

**YEAR-ROUND
SUMMER**

Size: 13" (33 cm)

Male: Small brown water bird with a black chin and black ring around a thick, chicken-like ivory bill. Puffy white patch under the tail. Has an unmarked brown bill during winter (September to February).

Female: same as male

Juvenile: paler than adult, with white spots and gray chest, belly and bill

Nest: floating platform; female and male build; 1 brood per year

Eggs: 5-7; bluish white without markings

Incubation: 22-24 days; female and male incubate

Fledging: 22-24 days; female and male feed young

Migration: complete, southern states, Mexico, Central America, non-migrator in parts of Idaho

Food: crayfish, aquatic insects, fish

Compare: The smallest brown water bird that dives underwater for long periods of time.

Stan's Notes: Common resident grebe, often seen diving for food. It slowly sinks like a submarine when disturbed. Formerly called Hell-diver because of the length of time it can stay submerged. Can surface far away from where it went under. Builds platform nest on a floating mat in water. Particularly sensitive to pollution. Adapted well to life on water, with short wings, lobed toes, and legs set close to the rear of body. While swimming is easy, it is very awkward on land. "Grebe" probably came from the Old English *krib*, meaning "crest," a reference to the Great Crested Grebe found in Europe.

male

female

SUMMER

CINNAMON TEAL
Anas cyanoptera

Size: 16" (40 cm)

Male: Deep cinnamon head, neck and belly. Light brown back. Dark gray bill. Deep red eyes. Non-breeding (July to September) male is overall brown with a red tinge.

Female: overall brown with a pale brown head, long shovel-like bill, green patch on wings

Juvenile: similar to female

Nest: ground; female builds; 1 brood per year

Eggs: 7-12; pinkish white without markings

Incubation: 21-25 days; female incubates

Fledging: 40-50 days; female teaches young to feed

Migration: partial to complete, to the U.S. West coast and Mexico

Food: aquatic plants and insects, seeds

Compare: Male Teal shares the cinnamon sides of the larger male Northern Shoveler (pg. 231), but lacks Shoveler's green head and very large spoon-shaped bill. Female Cinnamon Teal looks very similar to the smaller female Green-winged Teal (pg. 129), which has a dark line through the eyes.

Stan's Notes: The male teal is one of the most stunningly beautiful ducks. When threatened, the female feigns a wing injury to lure predators away from young. Prefers to nest along alkaline marshes and shallow lakes, within 75 yards (68 m) of water. Mallards and other ducks often lay eggs in teal nests, resulting in many nests totaling over 15 eggs.

male pg. 37

female

LESSER SCAUP
Aythya affinis

YEAR-ROUND
MIGRATION

Size: 16-17" (40-43 cm)

Female: Overall brown duck with dull white patch at base of light gray bill. Yellow eyes.

Male: white and gray, the chest and head appear nearly black but head appears purple with green highlights in direct sun, yellow eyes

Juvenile: same as female

Nest: ground; female builds; 1 brood per year

Eggs: 8-14; olive buff without markings

Incubation: 22-28 days; female incubates

Fledging: 45-50 days; female teaches young to feed

Migration: complete, to western coastal U.S., southern states, Mexico, Central America, northern South America

Food: aquatic plants and insects

Compare: Male Blue-winged Teal (pg. 131) is smaller, with a bright white crescent-shaped patch near base of bill. Smaller than female Wood Duck (pg. 139), which has white around the eyes, but lacks the white mark at base of bill. Look for the white patch at base of bill to help identify female Lesser Scaup.

Stan's Notes: A common diving duck. Often seen in large flocks on lakes, ponds and sewage lagoons. Completely submerges itself to feed on the bottom of lakes (unlike dabbling ducks, which only tip forward to reach bottom). Note the bold white stripe under the wings when in flight. Has an interesting baby-sitting arrangement in which groups of young are tended by one to three adult females.

RUFFED GROUSE
Bonasa umbellus

YEAR-ROUND

Size: 16-19" (40-48 cm)

Male: Brown chicken-like bird with long squared tail. Wide black band near tip of tail. Is able to fan tail like a turkey. Tuft of feathers on the head stands like a crown. Black ruffs on sides of neck.

Female: same as male, but less obvious neck ruffs

Juvenile: same as female

Nest: ground; female builds; 1 brood per year

Eggs: 9-12; tan with light brown markings

Incubation: 23-24 days; female incubates

Fledging: 10-12 days; female leads young to food

Migration: non-migrator

Food: seeds, insects, fruit, leaf buds

Compare: Smaller than the much darker female Blue Grouse (pg. 145), which has an obvious yellow comb. Look for a feathered tuft on the head and black neck ruffs.

Stan's Notes: A common bird of deep woods. Often seen in aspen or other trees, feeding on leaf buds. In the more northern climates, grows bristles on its feet during the winter to serve as snowshoes. When there is enough snow, it will dive into a snowbank to roost at night. In spring, male raises crest (tuft), fans tail feathers, and stands on logs and drums with wings to attract females. Drumming sound comes from cupped wings moving the air, not pounding on its chest or a log. Female will perform distraction display to protect young. Two color morphs, red and gray, most apparent in the tail. Black ruffs around the neck gave rise to its common name.

male pg. 229

female

WOOD DUCK
Aix sponsa

YEAR-ROUND
SUMMER

Size: 17-20" (43-50 cm)

Female: A small brown dabbling duck. Bright white eye-ring and a not-so-obvious crest. A blue patch on wing is often hidden.

Male: highly ornamented with a green head and crest patterned with white and black, rusty chest, white belly and red eyes

Juvenile: same as female

Nest: cavity; female lines old woodpecker cavity; 1 brood per year

Eggs: 10-15; creamy white without markings

Incubation: 28-36 days; female incubates

Fledging: 56-68 days; female teaches young to feed

Migration: complete, to southern states, partial to non-migrator in the northern Panhandle

Food: aquatic insects, plants, seeds

Compare: Smaller than the female Mallard (pg. 161) and similar to the female Blue-winged Teal (pg. 131). Mallard and Teal lack the female Duck's bright white eye-ring and crest.

Stan's Notes: A common duck of quiet, shallow backwater ponds. Nests in old woodpecker holes or in nest boxes. Often seen flying deep in forest or perched high on tree branches. Female takes flight with loud squealing call and enters nest cavity from full flight. Will lay eggs in a neighboring female nest (egg dumping), resulting in some clutches in excess of 20 eggs. Young stay in nest cavity only 24 hours after hatching, then jump from up to 30 feet (9 m) to the ground or water to follow their mother, never returning to the nest.

male

female

YEAR-ROUND
MIGRATION

Size: 19" (48 cm)

Male: A brown duck with a rounded head, a long pointed tail and short, black-tipped grayish bill. Obvious white cap. Deep green patch starting behind eyes, streaking down neck. White belly and wing linings, seen in flight. Non-breeding lacks white cap, green patch.

Female: light brown with a pale gray head, a short, black-tipped grayish bill, green wing patch (speculum), dark eye spot, white belly and wing linings, seen in flight

Juvenile: similar to female

Nest: ground; female builds; 1 brood per year

Eggs: 7-12; white without markings

Incubation: 23-25 days; female incubates

Fledging: 37-48 days; female teaches young to feed

Migration: partial migrator to non-migrator, along the West coast from Alaska to Mexico

Food: aquatic plants, seeds

Compare: The male Wigeon is easily identified by the white cap. Female Wigeon is similar to the female Cinnamon Teal (pg. 133), but has a short black-tipped bill and is less common.

Stan's Notes: Often in small flocks or with other ducks. Prefers shallow lakes. Male stays with female the first week of incubation only. Female raises young. If threatened, female feigns injury while young run and hide. Conceals upland nest in tall vegetation within 50 to 250 yards (46 to 228 m) of water.

male pg. 231

female

SWAINSON'S HAWK
Buteo swainsoni

MIGRATION
SUMMER

Size: 21" (53 cm); up to 4½-foot wingspan

Male: Highly variable-plumaged hawk with three easily distinguishable color morphs. Light morph is brown with a white belly, a warm rusty breast and a white face. Intermediate has a dark breast, rusty belly and white at the base of the bill. Dark morph is nearly all dark brown with a rusty color low on belly.

Female: same as male

Juvenile: similar to adult

Nest: platform; female and male build; 1 brood per year

Eggs: 2-4; bluish or white, some brown markings

Incubation: 28-35 days; female and male incubate

Fledging: 28-30 days; female and male feed young

Migration: complete, to Central and South America

Food: small mammals, insects, snakes, birds

Compare: The Red-tailed Hawk (pg. 149) has a white chest with brown belly band. Similar size as Rough-legged Hawk (pg. 151), but Rough-legged has a lighter trailing edge of wings.

Stan's Notes: A slender open country hawk that hunts mammals, insects, snakes and birds when soaring (kiting) or perching. Often flies with slightly upturned wings in a teetering, vulture-like flight. The light morph is the most common of the three color types, with intermediate and dark also common. Even minor nest disturbance can cause nest failure. Often gathers in large flocks to migrate.

soaring

RED-TAILED HAWK
Buteo jamaicensis

Size: 19-25" (48-63 cm); up to 4-foot wingspan

Male: Large hawk with amazing variety of colors from bird to bird, from chocolate brown to nearly all white. Often brown with a white breast and a distinctive brown belly band. Rust red tail usually only seen from above. Underside of wing is white with small dark patch on leading edge near shoulder.

Female: same as male, only slightly larger

Juvenile: similar to adults, lacking the red tail, has a speckled chest and light eyes

Nest: platform; male and female build; 1 brood per year

Eggs: 2-3; white without markings or sometimes marked with brown

Incubation: 30-35 days; female and male incubate

Fledging: 45-46 days; male and female feed young

Migration: non-migrator to partial migrator

Food: mice, birds, snakes, insects, mammals

Compare: Swainson's Hawk (pg. 147) is slimmer with longer, more pointed wings and longer tail.

Stan's Notes: A common hawk of open country and in cities in Idaho, frequently seen perched on freeway light posts, fences and trees. Look for it circling over open fields and roadsides, searching for prey. Their large stick nests are commonly seen in large trees along roads. Nests are lined with finer material such as evergreen tree needles. Will return to the same nest site each year. Doesn't develop red tail until the second year.

dark morph

soaring dark morph

light morph

soaring light morph

ROUGH-LEGGED HAWK
Buteo lagopus

Size: 22" (56 cm); up to 4½-foot wingspan

Male: A hawk of several plumages. All plumages have a long tail with a dark band or bands. Distinctive dark wrists and belly. Relatively long wings, small bill and feet. Light morph has nearly pure white undersides of wings and base of tail. Dark morph is nearly all brown with light gray trailing edge of wings.

Female: same as male, only larger

Juvenile: same as adults

Nest: platform, on edge of cliff; female and male build; 1 brood per year

Eggs: 2-6; white without markings

Incubation: 28-31 days; female and male incubate

Fledging: 39-43 days; female and male feed young

Migration: complete, to the northern half of the U.S.

Food: small animals, snakes, large insects

Compare: Similar size as Swainson's Hawk (pg. 147), which has narrow pointed wings, as seen in flight, and a lighter leading edge of wings, unlike Rough-legged's lighter trailing edge of wings.

Stan's Notes: Two color morphs, light and dark, light being more common. Common winter resident, nesting in Canada's Northwest Territories and Alaska. More numerous in some years than others. It has much smaller and weaker feet than the other birds of prey, which means it must hunt smaller prey. Hunts from the air, usually hovering before diving for small rodents such as mice and voles.

GREAT HORNED OWL
Bubo virginianus

YEAR-ROUND

Size: 20-25" (50-63 cm); up to 3½-foot wingspan

Male: Robust brown "horned" owl. Bright yellow eyes and V-shaped white throat resembling a necklace. Horizontal barring on the chest.

Female: same as male, only slightly larger

Juvenile: similar to adults, lacking ear tufts

Nest: no nest; takes over the nests of crows, Great Blue Herons and hawks, or will use partial cavities, stumps or broken-off trees; 1 brood per year

Eggs: 2; white without markings

Incubation: 26-30 days; female incubates

Fledging: 30-35 days; male and female feed young

Migration: non-migrator

Food: mammals, birds (ducks), snakes, insects

Compare: More than twice the size of its cousin, the Western Screech-Owl (pg. 191).

Stan's Notes: One of the earliest nesting birds in the state, laying eggs in January and February. Has excellent hearing; able to hear a mouse moving beneath a foot of snow. "Ears" are actually tufts of feathers (horns) and have nothing to do with hearing. Not able to turn its head all the way around. Wing feathers are ragged on ends, resulting in a silent flight. The eyelids close from the top down, like humans. Fearless, it is one of the few animals that will kill skunks and porcupines. Because of this, it is sometimes called Flying Tiger.

LONG-BILLED CURLEW
Numenius americanus

MIGRATION
SUMMER

Size: 23" (58 cm), including bill

Male: Cinnamon brown with an extremely long, down-curved bill. Long bluish legs. Darker cinnamon wing linings, seen in flight.

Female: same as male, but with a longer bill

Juvenile: same as adults, but with a shorter bill

Nest: ground; female builds; 1 brood per year

Eggs: 5-7; olive green with brown markings

Incubation: 27-30 days; female and male incubate, the female during day, male at night

Fledging: 32-45 days; female and male feed young

Migration: complete, to West coast states, Central and South American coasts

Food: insects, worms, crabs, eggs

Compare: Spotted Sandpiper (pg. 107) is smaller, less than half the size of the Long-billed Curlew. Hard to mistake the exceptionally long bill.

Stan's Notes: The largest of shorebirds, with an appropriate name. The extremely long bill is greater than half the length of its body. Females have longer bills than the males. Juveniles have short bills, which grow into long bills during the first six months. Uses its bill to probe deep into mud for insects and worms. Females incubate during the day, males during the night. Although a shorebird, it is often in grass fields away from the shore. Breeds in open valleys and flatland. Arrives in Idaho in April to begin nesting. Will fly as far as 6 miles (10 km) from the nest site to find food. Decreasing in Idaho due to agriculture, which destroys its nesting habitat.

male pg. 211

female

NORTHERN HARRIER
Circus cyaneus

YEAR-ROUND

Size: 24" (60 cm); up to 3½-foot wingspan

Female: A slim, low-flying hawk. Dark brown back with brown-streaked breast and belly. Large white rump patch and narrow black bands across tail. Tips of wings black. Yellow eyes.

Male: silver gray with large white rump patch and white belly, faint narrow bands across tail, tips of wings black, yellow eyes

Juvenile: similar to female, with an orange breast

Nest: platform, often on ground; female and male build; 1 brood per year

Eggs: 4-8; bluish white without markings

Incubation: 31-32 days; female incubates

Fledging: 30-35 days; male and female feed young

Migration: partial migrator, to western coastal U.S., southern states, Mexico, Central America, non-migrator in Idaho

Food: mice, snakes, insects, small birds

Compare: Slimmer than Red-tailed Hawk (pg. 149). Look for black bands on tail and a white rump patch.

Stan's Notes: One of the easiest hawks to identify. Harriers glide just above ground, following contours of the land while searching for prey. Holds its wings just above the horizontal position, tilting back and forth in the wind, similar to Turkey Vultures. Formerly called Marsh Hawk due to its habit of hunting over marshes. Feeds on the ground. Will perch on the ground to preen and rest. At any age, has a distinctive owl-like face disk.

male

female

NORTHERN PINTAIL
Anas acuta

Size: 26" (66 cm), male
21" (53 cm), female

Male: A slender, elegant duck with a brown head, white neck, gray body and extremely long, narrow black tail. Gray bill. Non-breeding has a pale brown head that lacks the clear demarcation between the brown head and white neck. Lacks long tail feathers.

Female: mottled brown body with a paler head and neck, long tail, gray bill

Juvenile: similar to female

Nest: ground; female builds; 1 brood per year

Eggs: 6-9; olive green without markings

Incubation: 22-25 days; female incubates

Fledging: 36-50 days; female teaches young to feed

Migration: partial to non-migrator, to western coastal U.S., southern states and Mexico

Food: aquatic plants and insects, seeds

Compare: The male Northern Pintail has a distinctive brown head and white neck. Look for the unique long tail feathers. The female Pintail is similar to female Mallard (pg. 161), but Mallard has an orange bill with black spots.

Stan's Notes: A common duck of marshes in the state. About 90 percent of its diet is aquatic plants, except when the females feed heavily on aquatic insects just prior to nesting, presumably to gain extra nutrients for egg production.

male pg. 235

female

MALLARD
Anas platyrhynchos

YEAR-ROUND

Size: 27-28" (69-71 cm)

Female: All brown with orange and black bill. Small blue and white wing mark (speculum).

Male: large, bulbous green head, white necklace, rust brown or chestnut chest, combination of gray and white on the sides, yellow bill, orange legs and feet

Juvenile: same as female, but with a yellow bill

Nest: ground; female builds; 1 brood per year

Eggs: 7-10; greenish to whitish, unmarked

Incubation: 26-30 days; female incubates

Fledging: 42-52 days; female leads young to food

Migration: partial migrator to non-migrator in Idaho

Food: seeds, plants, aquatic insects; will come to ground feeders offering corn

Compare: The female Northern Shoveler (pg. 143) is smaller and has a large spoon-shaped bill. The female Wood Duck (pg. 139) is also smaller, with a white eye-ring. The female Northern Pintail (pg. 159) is similar, with a gray bill.

Stan's Notes: A familiar duck of lakes and ponds, it's considered a type of dabbling duck, tipping forward in shallow water to feed on aquatic plants on the bottom. The name "Mallard" comes from the Latin *masculus*, meaning "male," referring to the habit of males not taking part in raising ducklings. Both female and male have white tails and white underwings. Black central tail feathers of male curl upward. Will return to place of birth.

161

male

female

RING-NECKED PHEASANT
Phasianus colchicus

YEAR-ROUND

Size: 30-36" (76-90 cm), male, including tail
21-25" (53-63 cm), female, including tail

Male: Golden brown body with a long tail. White ring around neck with purple, green, blue and red head.

Female: smaller, less flamboyant all-brown bird with a long tail

Juvenile: similar to female, with a shorter tail

Nest: ground; female builds; 1 brood per year

Eggs: 8-10; olive brown without markings

Incubation: 23-25 days; female incubates

Fledging: 11-12 days; female leads young to food

Migration: non-migrator

Food: insects, seeds, fruit; visits ground feeders

Compare: The female Blue Grouse (pg. 145) is smaller than the female Ring-necked and lacks the long tail. Much larger than California Quail (pg. 197) and lacks a teardrop plume on the forehead. Male Ring-necked Pheasant is brightly colored.

Stan's Notes: Introduced from China in the late 1800s. Common now across the U.S. Like many other game birds, their numbers vary greatly, making them common in some years and scarce in others. "Ring-necked" refers to the thin white ring around the male's neck. "Pheasant" comes from the Greek word *phaisianos*, meaning "bird of the River Phasis." (The Phasis, located in Europe, is now known as the River Rioni.) Listen for the male's cackling call to attract females.

soaring

juvenile

GOLDEN EAGLE
Aquila chrysaetos

Size: 30-40" (76-102 cm); up to 7-foot wingspan

Male: Uniform dark brown with golden head and nape of neck. Yellow around the base of bill and yellow feet.

Female: same as male

Juvenile: similar to adult, but has white wrist patches and white base of tail

Nest: platform, on cliff; female and male build; 1 brood per year

Eggs: 2; white with brown markings

Incubation: 43-45 days; female and male incubate

Fledging: 66-75 days; female and male feed young

Migration: non-migrator to partial migrator; will move around to find food

Food: mammals, birds, reptiles, insects

Compare: Similar to Bald Eagle (pg. 49), lacking the white head and tail. Juvenile Golden Eagle, with its white wrist marks and base of tail, is often confused with juvenile Bald Eagle.

Stan's Notes: Large and powerful bird of prey that has no trouble taking larger prey such as jack rabbits. Hunts by perching or soaring and watching for movement. Inhabits mountainous terrain, requiring large territories to provide large supply of food. Thought to mate for life, renewing pair bond late in winter with spectacular high-flying courtship displays. Usually nests on cliff faces, rarely in trees. Uses well-established nest that has been used for generations. Not uncommon for it to add things to nest such as antlers, bones and barbed wire.

WILD TURKEY
Meleagris gallopavo

Size: 36-48" (90-120 cm)

Male: Large, plump brown and bronze bird with striking blue and red bare head. Fan tail and long, straight black beard in center of chest. Spurs on legs.

Female: thinner and less striking than male, usually lacking breast beard

Juvenile: same as adult of the same sex

Nest: ground; female builds; 1 brood per year

Eggs: 10-12; buff white with dull brown markings

Incubation: 27-28 days; female incubates

Fledging: 6-10 days; female leads young to food

Migration: non-migrator

Food: insects, seeds, fruit

Compare: This bird is quite distinctive and unlikely to be confused with others.

Stan's Notes: The largest game bird in Idaho, and the bird from which the domestic turkey was bred. Almost became our national bird, losing to the Bald Eagle by a single vote. Strong fliers, they can approach 60 miles (97 km) per hour. Able to fly straight up, then away. Eyesight is three times better than human eyesight. Hearing is also excellent; can hear competing males up to a mile away. Males hold "harems" of up to 20 females. Males are called toms, females are hens and young are poults. At night, they roost in trees.

RUBY-CROWNED KINGLET
Regulus calendula

YEAR-ROUND
SUMMER

Size: 4" (10 cm)

Male: Small, teardrop-shaped green-to-gray bird. Two white wing bars. Hidden ruby-colored crown. White eye-ring.

Female: same as male, but lacking the ruby crown

Juvenile: same as female

Nest: pendulous; female builds; 1 brood per year

Eggs: 4-5; white with brown markings

Incubation: 11-12 days; female incubates

Fledging: 11-12 days; female and male feed young

Migration: complete, southern states, Mexico, Central America, partial migrator in Idaho

Food: insects, berries

Compare: The female American Goldfinch (pg. 265) is larger, but shares the same olive color and unmarked breast. Look for the white eye-ring of Ruby-crowned Kinglet.

Stan's Notes: One of the smaller birds in the state, it takes a quick eye to see the male's ruby crown. Most commonly seen during the spring and fall migrations, when groups travel together. Look for it flitting around thick shrubs low to the ground. Female builds an unusual pendulous (sac-like) nest, intricately woven and decorated on the outside with colored lichens and mosses stuck together with spider webs. The nest is suspended from a branch overlapped by leaves and usually is hung high in a mature tree. The common name "Kinglet" comes from the Anglo-Saxon word *cyning*, or "king," referring to the male's ruby crown, and the diminutive suffix "let," meaning "small."

PYGMY NUTHATCH
Sitta pygmaea

YEAR-ROUND

Size: 4¼" (10.5 cm)

Male: Tiny gray-blue black bird with gray-brown crown. Creamy chest with a lighter chin. A relatively short tail, large head and long bill.

Female: same as male

Juvenile: same as adult

Nest: cavity; the female and male build; 1 brood per year

Eggs: 4-8; white with brown markings

Incubation: 14-16 days; female incubates

Fledging: 20-22 days; female and male feed young

Migration: non-migrator

Food: insects, berries, seeds; will visit seed feeders

Compare: Smaller than the Red-breasted Nuthatch (pg. 173) and the White-breasted Nuthatch (pg. 181). The Red-breasted has a rusty red chest, compared with the creamy breast of the Pygmy. White-breasted has a distinctive black cap and a white chest.

Stan's Notes: A bird of Ponderosa Pine forest in the Panhandle. Unlike White-breasted Nuthatch, Pygmy Nuthatch needs mature ponderosas with old or decaying wood. Usually drills its own nest cavity. While it doesn't migrate, it forms winter flocks with other birds, such as chickadees and creepers, and moves around to find food. Usually feeds in a crown of a tree or at the ends of twigs and branches where it searches for insects and seeds, unlike the White-breasted and Red-breasted Nuthatches, which usually search trunks of trees for food.

171

RED-BREASTED NUTHATCH
Sitta canadensis

YEAR-ROUND

Size: 4½" (11 cm)

Male: A small gray-backed bird with a black cap and a prominent eye line. A rust red breast and belly.

Female: gray cap, pale undersides

Juvenile: same as female

Nest: cavity; female builds; 1 brood per year

Eggs: 5-6; white with red brown markings

Incubation: 11-12 days; female incubates

Fledging: 14-20 days; female and male feed young

Migration: non-migrator to irruptive; moves around the state in search of food

Food: insects, seeds; visits seed and suet feeders

Compare: Slightly larger than the Pygmy Nuthatch (pg. 171) and smaller than White-breasted Nuthatch (pg. 181), neither of which has the rich red breast of the Red-breasted.

Stan's Notes: Red-breasted Nuthatch behaves like White-breasted and Pygmy Nuthatches, climbing down trunks of trees headfirst. Similar to chickadees, visits seed feeders, quickly grabbing a seed and flying off to crack it open. Will wedge a seed into a crevice and pound it open with several sharp blows. The name "Nuthatch" comes from the Middle English moniker *nuthak*, referring to the bird's habit of wedging a seed into a crevice and hacking it open. Look for it in mature conifers, frequently extracting seeds from cones. Doesn't excavate a cavity as the chickadee might; rather, it takes over a former woodpecker or chickadee cavity.

BLACK-CAPPED CHICKADEE
Poecile atricapilla

YEAR-ROUND

Size: 5" (13 cm)

Male: Familiar gray bird with black cap and throat patch. White chest. Tan belly. Small white wing marks.

Female: same as male

Juvenile: same as adult

Nest: cavity; female and male build or excavate; 1 brood per year

Eggs: 5-7; white with fine brown markings

Incubation: 11-13 days; female and male incubate

Fledging: 14-18 days; female and male feed young

Migration: non-migrator

Food: insects, seeds, fruit; comes to seed and suet feeders

Compare: Similar to Mountain and Chestnut-backed Chickadees (pp. 177 and 65, respectively). Mountain Chickadee has white eyebrows, and the Chestnut-backed has a distinctive chestnut-colored back.

Stan's Notes: Backyard bird that is attracted to a nest box or seed feeder. Usually the first to find a new feeder. Can be easily tamed and hand fed. Can be a common urban bird since much of its diet comes from bird feeders. Needs to feed each day in winter; forages for food during even the worst winter storms. Often seen with other birds such as nuthatches and woodpeckers. Builds its nest mostly with green moss and lines it with animal fur. Name comes from its familiar "chika-dee-dee-dee-dee" call. Also gives a high-pitched, two-toned "fee-bee" call. Can have different calls in various regions.

MOUNTAIN CHICKADEE
Poecile gambeli

Size: 5½" (14 cm)

Male: Overall gray with a black cap, chin and line through the eyes. White eyebrows.

Female: same as male

Juvenile: similar to adult

Nest: cavity, old woodpecker hole or excavates its own; female and male build; 1-2 broods per year

Eggs: 5-8; white without markings

Incubation: 11-14 days; female and male incubate

Fledging: 18-21 days; female and male feed young

Migration: partial migrator

Food: seeds, insects; visits seed and suet feeders

Compare: The Black-capped Chickadee (pg. 175) is similar, but lacks the white eyebrows of the Mountain Chickadee.

Stan's Notes: An abundant bird in the state, but more common in coniferous forests in mountainous regions of Idaho, preferring old growth spruce, fir and Lodgepole Pine forests. Feeds heavily on coniferous seeds and insects. Usually will not mingle with Black-capped Chickadees, but does flock with other birds in the winter. Moves to lower elevations in winter, returning to high elevations for nesting. Excavates a nest cavity or uses an old woodpecker hole. Will use a nest box. Occasionally uses same nest site year after year. Lines its nest with moss, hair and feathers. Female won't leave nest if disturbed, but will hiss and flutter wings.

female
pg. 77

male

Oregon male

DARK-EYED JUNCO
Junco hyemalis

Size: 5½" (14 cm)

Male: A round, dark-eyed bird with slate-gray-to-charcoal chest, head and back. White belly. Pink bill. Since the outermost tail feathers are white, tail appears as a white V in flight.

Female: same as male, only tan-to-brown color

Juvenile: similar to female, but has a streaked breast and head

Nest: cup; female and male build; 2 broods a year

Eggs: 3-5; white with reddish brown markings

Incubation: 12-13 days; female incubates

Fledging: 10-13 days; male and female feed young

Migration: partial migrator to complete, across the U.S.

Food: seeds, insects; will come to seed feeders

Compare: Rarely confused with any other bird. Small flocks feed under bird feeders in winter.

Stan's Notes: Several junco species have now been combined into one, simply called Dark-eyed Junco (see lower inset). A common year-round resident. One of the most numerous wintering birds in the state, spending winters in foothills and plains after snowmelt, returning to higher elevations for nesting. Nests in a wide variety of wooded habitats in April and May. Usually is seen on the ground in small flocks. It adheres to a rigid social hierarchy, with dominant birds chasing the less dominant birds. Look for its white outer tail feathers flashing in flight. Most comfortable on the ground, juncos will "double-scratch" with both feet to expose seeds and insects. Consumes many weed seeds.

WHITE-BREASTED NUTHATCH
Sitta carolinensis

Size: 5-6" (13-15 cm)

Male: Slate gray with a white face and belly, and black cap and nape. Long thin bill, slightly upturned. Chestnut undertail.

Female: similar to male, gray cap and nape

Juvenile: similar to female

Nest: cavity; the female and male build; 1 brood per year

Eggs: 5-7; white with brown markings

Incubation: 11-12 days; female incubates

Fledging: 13-14 days; female and male feed young

Migration: non-migrator

Food: insects, seeds; visits seed and suet feeders

Compare: Red-breasted Nuthatch (pg. 173) is smaller, with a rusty belly and distinctive black eye line. Pygmy Nuthatch (pg. 171) is smaller and lacks the White-breasted's black cap.

Stan's Notes: The nuthatch's habit of hopping headfirst down tree trunks helps it see insects and insect eggs that birds climbing up the trunk might miss. Incredible climbing agility comes from an extra-long hind toe claw or nail, nearly twice the size of the front toe claws. The name "Nuthatch" comes from the Middle English moniker *nuthak*, referring to the bird's habit of wedging a seed into a crevice and hacking it open. Often seen in mixed flocks of Brown Creepers, chickadees and Downy Woodpeckers. Mated pairs stay together all year, defending small territories. Listen for its characteristic springtime call, "whi-whi-whi-whi," given in February and March. One of 17 worldwide nuthatch species.

male

female

YELLOW-RUMPED WARBLER
Dendroica coronata

YEAR-ROUND
SUMMER

Size: 5-6" (13-15 cm)

Male: Slate gray bird with black mask and breast. Yellow patch on the head, flanks and rump. White chin and belly. Two white wing bars.

Female: duller than male, but same yellow patches

Juvenile: similar to female

Nest: cup; female builds; 2 broods per year

Eggs: 4-5; white with brown markings

Incubation: 12-13 days; female incubates

Fledging: 10-12 days; female and male feed young

Migration: complete, to southern states, Mexico and Central America

Food: insects, berries; rarely comes to suet feeders

Compare: The Common Yellowthroat (pg. 267) has a yellow breast, unlike the Yellow-rumped's patches of yellow. The male Yellow Warbler (pg. 271) is all yellow with orange streaks on breast. Male Wilson's Warbler (pg. 263) has a characteristic black crown. Look for a combination of yellow patches on the head, flanks and rump.

Stan's Notes: A common warbler in Idaho, nesting in coniferous and aspen forests. Flocks of hundreds seen during migration in the fall, usually arriving in late September to early October. Male molts to a dull color in winter similar to the female, retaining the yellow patches. Sometimes called Butter-butts due to the yellow patch on rump. Formerly called Audubon's or Myrtle Warbler. Familiar call is a robust "chip."

WESTERN WOOD-PEWEE
Contopus sordidulus

Size: 6¼" (15.5 cm)

Male: An overall gray bird with darker wings and tail. Two narrow gray wing bars. Dull white throat with pale yellow or white belly. Black upper bill, dull orange lower.

Female: same as male

Juvenile: similar to adult, lacking the two-toned bill

Nest: cup; female builds; 1 brood per year

Eggs: 2-4; pale white with brown markings

Incubation: 12-14 days; female incubates

Fledging: 14-18 days; female and male feed young

Migration: complete, to Central and South America

Food: insects

Compare: This is an unremarkable bird. Look for the Wood-Pewee's distinctive gray wing bars to help identify.

Stan's Notes: A widespread bird in the state that is most common in aspen forests and near water. It requires trees with dead tops or branches from which to sing and hunt for flying insects, which compose nearly all of the diet. Often returns to the same perch after each foray. Nests throughout western North America from Alaska to Mexico. Overall populations are decreasing about 1 percent each year. Common name comes from a nasal whistle, "pee-wee."

AMERICAN DIPPER
Cinclus mexicanus

Size: 7½" (19 cm)

Male: Dark gray to black overall, slightly lighter-colored head. Short upturned tail and dark eyes and bill.

Female: same as male

Juvenile: similar to adult, only paler with white eyelids that are most noticeable when blinking

Nest: pendulous, covered nest with the entrance near the bottom, on cliff, behind waterfall; female builds; 1-2 broods per year

Eggs: 3-5; white without markings

Incubation: 13-17 days; female incubates

Fledging: 18-25 days; female and male feed young

Migration: non-migrator; seeks moving open water

Food: aquatic insects, small fish, crustaceans

Compare: Similar shape as American Robin (pg. 195), but lacks a red breast. The only songbird in Idaho that dives into fast-moving water.

Stan's Notes: A common bird of fast, usually noisy streams that provide some kind of protected shelf on which to construct a nest. Some have had success attracting with man-made ledges. Plunges headfirst into fast-moving water, looking for just about any aquatic insect, propelling itself underwater with its wings. Frequently seen emerging with a large insect, which it smashes against rock before eating. Depending on snowmelt, nesting usually starts in March or April. American Dippers in lower elevations often nest for a second time each season.

EASTERN KINGBIRD
Tyrannus tyrannus

SUMMER

Size: 8" (20 cm)

Male: Mostly black gray bird with white belly and chin. Black head and tail with a distinctive white band across the end of the tail. Has a concealed red crown that is rarely seen.

Female: same as male

Juvenile: same as adult

Nest: cup; male and female build; 1 brood a year

Eggs: 3-4; white with brown markings

Incubation: 16-18 days; female incubates

Fledging: 16-18 days; female and male feed young

Migration: complete, to Mexico, Central America and South America

Food: insects, fruit

Compare: Rarely confused with other birds. Lacks any yellow of the Western Kingbird (pg. 281). Medium-sized bird, smaller than American Robin (pg. 195). Look for the white band along the end of the tail to identify.

Stan's Notes: A common bird throughout Idaho in open fields and prairies. Fall migration begins in late August and early September, with groups of up to 20 individuals migrating together. Returns to the mating ground in springtime, where male and female defend their territory. Acting unafraid of other birds and chasing the larger ones, it is perceived as having an attitude. Bold behavior gave rise to the common name, King. Perches on tall branches, watching for insects. After flying out to catch them, returns to the same perch, a technique called hawking.

gray morph

brown morph

WESTERN SCREECH-OWL
Otus kennicottii

YEAR-ROUND

Size:	8½" (22 cm); up to 1½-foot wingspan
Male:	A small, overall gray owl with bright yellow eyes. Two short ear tufts. A short tail. Some birds are brownish.
Female:	same as male
Juvenile:	similar to adult of the same morph, lacks ear tufts
Nest:	cavity; uses old woodpecker hole; 1 brood per year
Eggs:	2-6; white without markings
Incubation:	21-30 days; female incubates
Fledging:	25-30 days; female and male feed young
Migration:	non-migrator
Food:	insects, small mammals, birds
Compare:	Less than half the size of the Great Horned Owl (pg. 153), it is hard to confuse with its considerably larger cousin.

Stan's Notes: The most common small owl throughout Idaho. An owl of suburban woodlands and backyards. Requires trees that are at least a foot in diameter for nesting and roosting, so it usually is found in towns or in trees that have been preserved. A secondary cavity nester, which means it nests in tree cavities created by other birds. Usually not found in elevations above 4,000 feet (1,200 m). Densities in lower elevations are about 1 bird per square mile (2 to 3 per sq. km). Most screech-owls are gray; some are brown.

LOGGERHEAD SHRIKE
Lanius ludovicianus

Size: 9" (22.5 cm)

Male: A gray head and back with black wings and mask across the eyes. A white chin, breast and belly. Black tail, legs and feet. Black bill with hooked tip. White wing patches, seen in flight.

Female: same as male

Juvenile: dull version of adult

Nest: cup; the male and female build; 1-2 broods per year

Eggs: 4-7; off-white with dark markings

Incubation: 16-17 days; female incubates

Fledging: 17-21 days; female and male feed young

Migration: complete, to southern states, Mexico, non-migrator in southern third of Idaho

Food: insects, lizards, small mammals, frogs

Compare: Distinctive-looking bird. Look for the black wings and mask across the eyes to help identify. Cedar Waxwing (pg. 103) also has a black mask, but is brown, not gray and black like the Shrike.

Stan's Notes: The Loggerhead is a songbird that acts like a bird of prey. Known for skewering prey on barbed wire fences, thorns and other sharp objects to store or hold still while tearing apart to eat, hence its other common name, Butcher Bird. Feet are too weak to hold the prey it eats. Breeding bird surveys indicate declining populations in the Great Plains due to pesticides killing its major food source–grasshoppers.

male

female

AMERICAN ROBIN
Turdus migratorius

Size: 9-11" (22.5-28 cm)

Male: A familiar gray bird with a rusty red breast, and nearly black head and tail. White chin with black streaks. White eye-ring.

Female: similar to male, but with a gray head and a duller breast

Juvenile: similar to female, but has a speckled breast and brown back

Nest: cup; female builds with help from the male; 2-3 broods per year

Eggs: 4-7; pale blue without markings

Incubation: 12-14 days; female incubates

Fledging: 14-16 days; female and male feed young

Migration: complete, southern states, Mexico, Central America, non-migrator in parts of Idaho

Food: insects, fruit, berries, worms

Compare: Familiar bird to all.

Stan's Notes: Although a complete migrator in northern states, it is a year-round resident in parts of Idaho. Can be heard singing all night long during springtime. Most people don't realize how easy it is to differentiate between the male and female robins. Compare the male's dark, nearly black head and brick red breast with the female's gray head and dull red breast. Robins are not listening for worms when they cock their heads to one side. They are looking with eyes that are placed far back on the sides of their heads. A very territorial bird. Often seen fighting its own reflection in windows.

male

female

YEAR-ROUND

CLARK'S NUTCRACKER
Nucifraga columbiana

Size: 12" (30 cm)

Male: Gray with black wings and a narrow black band down the center of tail. Small white patches on long wings, seen in flight. Has a relatively short tail with a white undertail.

Female: same as male

Juvenile: same as adult

Nest: cup; female and male build; 1 brood a year

Eggs: 2-5; pale green with brown markings

Incubation: 16-18 days; female and male incubate

Fledging: 18-20 days; female and male feed young

Migration: non-migrator

Food: seeds, insects, berries, eggs, mammals

Compare: Slightly larger than the Gray Jay (pg. 199), which lacks the Nutcracker's black wings. The Steller's Jay (pg. 61) is dark blue with a black crest.

Stan's Notes: A high country bird found in coniferous forests in most of Idaho. While it has a varied diet, it relies heavily on piñon seeds, often caching large amounts to consume later or feed young. Has a large pouch in its throat (sublingual pouch), which it uses to transport seeds. Studies show the birds can carry up to 100 seeds at a time. Nests early in the year, often while snow still covers the ground, relying on stored foods.

soaring

juvenile

SHARP-SHINNED HAWK
Accipiter striatus

Size: 10-14" (25-36 cm); up to 2-foot wingspan

Male: Small woodland hawk with gray back and head, and rusty red breast. Long tail with several dark tail bands, widest band at end of squared-off tail. Red eyes.

Female: same as male, only larger

Juvenile: same size as adults, with a brown back and heavily streaked breast, yellow eyes

Nest: platform; female builds; 1 brood per year

Eggs: 4-5; white with brown markings

Incubation: 32-35 days; female incubates

Fledging: 24-27 days; female and male feed young

Migration: complete, southern states, Mexico, Central America, non-migrator in parts of Idaho

Food: birds, small mammals

Compare: Nearly identical to Cooper's Hawk (pg. 207), only smaller. Look for the Sharp-shinned's squared tail, compared with the rounded tail of the Cooper's.

Stan's Notes: A common hawk of backyards and woodlands, often seen swooping in on birds visiting feeders. Its short rounded wings and long tail allow this hawk to navigate through thick stands of trees in pursuit of prey. Common name comes from the sharp keel on the leading edge of its "shin," though it is actually below rather than above the bird's ankle on the tarsus bone of foot. The tarsus in most birds is round. In flight, head doesn't protrude as far as the head of the Cooper's Hawk.

ROCK DOVE
Columba livia

YEAR-ROUND

Size: 13" (33 cm)

Male: No set color pattern. Gray to white, patches of iridescent greens and blues, usually with a light rump patch.

Female: same as male

Juvenile: same as adult

Nest: platform; female builds; 3-4 broods a year

Eggs: 1-2; white without markings

Incubation: 18-20 days; female and male incubate

Fledging: 25-26 days; female and male feed young

Migration: non-migrator

Food: seeds

Compare: The Mourning Dove (pg. 125) is smaller and light brown in color.

Stan's Notes: Also known as Domestic Pigeon, it was introduced to North America from Europe by the early settlers. Most common around cities and barnyards, where it scratches for seeds. One of the few birds that has a wide variety of colors, produced by years of selective breeding while in captivity. Parents feed their young a regurgitated liquid known as crop-milk for the first few days of life. One of the few birds that can drink without tilting its head back. Nests under bridges and on buildings, balconies, barns and sheds. Was once poisoned as a "nuisance city bird." Many cities now have Peregrine Falcons (not shown) that feed on Rock Doves, keeping their numbers in check.

soaring

juvenile

COOPER'S HAWK
Accipiter cooperii

Size: 14-20" (36-50 cm); up to 2½-foot wingspan

Male: Medium-sized hawk with short wings and long rounded tail with several black bands. Rusty breast and dark wing tips. Slate gray back. Bright yellow spot at base of gray bill (cere). Dark red eyes.

Female: similar to male, only slightly larger

Juvenile: brown back with brown streaks on breast, bright yellow eyes

Nest: platform; male and female build; 1 brood per year

Eggs: 2-4; greenish with brown markings

Incubation: 32-36 days; female and male incubate

Fledging: 28-32 days; male and female feed young

Migration: complete, to southern states and Mexico, non-migrator in parts of Idaho

Food: small birds, mammals

Compare: Nearly identical to the Sharp-shinned Hawk (pg. 203), only larger, darker gray and with a rounded-off tail.

Stan's Notes: A resident hawk in Idaho woodlands. In flight, look for its large head, short wings and long tail. The short stubby wings help it maneuver between trees while pursuing small birds. Will come to feeders, hunting for unaware birds. Flies with long glides followed by a few quick flaps. Known to ambush prey, it will fly into heavy brush or even run on the ground in pursuit. Nestlings have gray eyes that become bright yellow at 1 year of age and dark red later.

YEAR-ROUND

female pg. 145

male

BLUE GROUSE
Dendragapus obscurus

YEAR-ROUND

Size: 20" (50 cm)

Male: Dark gray chicken-like bird. Bright yellow-to-orange patch of skin above eyes (comb). While displaying, white feathers surround an inflated yellow or purplish sac. Fans a gray-tipped, nearly black tail.

Female: mottled brown, gray belly, yellow patch of skin above eyes (comb)

Juvenile: similar to female

Nest: ground; female builds; 1 brood per year

Eggs: 6-12; pale white with brown markings

Incubation: 24-26 days; female incubates

Fledging: 7-10 days; female feeds young

Migration: non-migrator to partial migrator; will move around to find food

Food: insects, seeds, fruit, leaf buds and coniferous needles (Douglas-fir)

Compare: Larger than Ruffed Grouse (pg. 137). Look for male's obvious yellow-to-orange comb.

Stan's Notes: A common grouse seen from foothills to timberline. Usually on the ground, but also seen in trees feeding upon newly opened leaf buds in spring. Often switches from an insect diet in summer to coniferous needles in winter. Male engages in elaborate courtship displays by fanning its tail, inflating its bright neck sac and singing (calling). Male mates with several females. Young leave nests within 24 hours and follow their mothers to feed. Very tame and freezes when threatened, making it easy to get a close look.

male

female pg. 157

NORTHERN HARRIER
Circus cyaneus

YEAR-ROUND

Size: 24" (60 cm); up to 3½-foot wingspan

Male: A slim, low-flying hawk. Silver gray with a large white rump patch and a white belly. Faint narrow bands across the tail. Tips of wings black. Yellow eyes.

Female: dark brown back, a brown-streaked breast and belly, large white rump patch, narrow black bands across tail, tips of wings black, yellow eyes

Juvenile: similar to female, with an orange breast

Nest: platform, often on ground; female and male build; 1 brood per year

Eggs: 4-8; bluish white without markings

Incubation: 31-32 days; female incubates

Fledging: 30-35 days; male and female feed young

Migration: partial migrator, to southern states, Mexico, Central America, non-migrator in Idaho

Food: mice, snakes, insects, small birds

Compare: Slimmer than Red-tailed Hawk (pg. 149). Look for black bands on tail and a white rump patch.

Stan's Notes: One of the easiest hawks to identify. Harriers glide just above ground, following contours of the land while searching for prey. Holds its wings just above the horizontal position, tilting back and forth in the wind, similar to Turkey Vultures. Formerly called Marsh Hawk due to its habit of hunting over marshes. Feeds on the ground. Will perch on the ground to preen and rest. At any age, has a distinctive owl-like face disk.

CANADA GOOSE
Branta canadensis

YEAR-ROUND

Size: 25-43" (63-109 cm)

Male: Large gray goose with black neck and head, with a white chin or cheek strap.

Female: same as male

Juvenile: same as adult

Nest: platform, on the ground; female builds; 1 brood per year

Eggs: 5-10; white without markings

Incubation: 25-30 days; female incubates

Fledging: 42-55 days; male and female teach young to feed

Migration: non-migrator

Food: aquatic plants, insects, seeds

Compare: Large goose that is rarely confused with any other bird.

Stan's Notes: Common year-round residents throughout the state. Adults mate for many years, but only start to breed in their third year. Males often act as sentinels, standing at the edge of a group, bobbing their heads up and down, becoming very aggressive to anybody who approaches. Will hiss as if displaying displeasure. Adults molt primary flight feathers while raising young, rendering family groups flightless at the same time. Several subspecies vary geographically around the U.S. Generally they are darker in color in western groups and paler in eastern. Size decreases northward, with the smallest subspecies found on the Arctic tundra.

SANDHILL CRANE
Grus canadensis

Size: 40-48" (102-120 cm); up to 7-foot wingspan

Male: Elegant gray bird with long legs and neck. Wings and body often stained rusty brown. Scarlet red cap. Yellow-to-red eyes.

Female: same as male

Juvenile: dull brown, lacks red cap, has yellow eyes

Nest: platform, on the ground; female and male build; 1 brood per year

Eggs: 2; olive with brown markings

Incubation: 28-32 days; female and male incubate

Fledging: 65 days; female and male feed young

Migration: complete, to southern states and Mexico

Food: insects, fruit, worms, plants, amphibians

Compare: Similar size as Great Blue Heron (pg. 217), but the Crane has a shorter bill and red cap. Great Blue Heron flies with neck held in an S shape, unlike the Crane's straight neck.

Stan's Notes: Among the tallest birds in the world and capable of flying at great heights. Usually seen in large undisturbed fields near water. Often heard before seen, they have a very distinctive rattling call. Plumage often appears rust brown because of staining from mud during preening. Characteristic flight with upstroke quicker than down. For their spectacular mating dance the performers face each other, bow and jump into the air while uttering loud cackling sounds and flapping wings. Often flips sticks and grass into the air during dance.

GREAT BLUE HERON
Ardea herodias

YEAR-ROUND
SUMMER

Size: 42-52" (107-132 cm)

Male: Tall gray heron. Black eyebrows extend into several long plumes off the back of head. Long yellow bill. Feathers at base of neck drop down in a kind of necklace.

Female: same as male

Juvenile: same as adult, but more brown than gray, with a black crown and no plumes

Nest: platform; male and female build; 1 brood per year

Eggs: 3-5; blue green without markings

Incubation: 27-28 days; female and male incubate

Fledging: 56-60 days; male and female feed young

Migration: complete, southern states, Mexico, Central America, South America, partial migrator, to southern Idaho

Food: small fish, frogs, insects, snakes

Compare: Similar size as the Sandhill Crane (pg. 215), but lacks the Crane's red crown. Crane flies with neck held straight, unlike the Heron's S-shaped neck.

Stan's Notes: One of the most common herons, often barking like a dog when startled. Seen stalking small fish in shallow water. Will strike at mice, squirrels and just about anything else it might come across. Flies holding neck in an S shape, with its long legs trailing straight out behind. The wings are held in cupped fashion during flight. Nests in colonies of up to 100 birds. Nests in treetops near or over open water.

male

female

CALLIOPE HUMMINGBIRD
Stellula calliope

Size: 3¼" (8 cm)

Male: Iridescent green head, back and tail. Breast and belly white to tan. Iridescent rosy red throat patch (gorget), V-shaped. Compared with other hummingbirds, has a very short, thin bill and a short tail. Wing tips reach to tip of tail.

Female: same as male, but thin, spotty throat patch

Juvenile: similar to female

Nest: cup; female builds; 1 brood per year

Eggs: 1-2; white without markings

Incubation: 15-17 days; female incubates

Fledging: 18-22 days; female feeds young

Migration: complete, to Central and South America

Food: nectar, insects; will come to nectar feeders

Compare: Smaller than other hummingbirds. Look for the short thin bill and short tail. Broad-tailed Hummingbird (pg. 221) is very similar with a slightly longer tail. Female is similar to the female Rufous Hummingbird (pg. 237), but has a shorter, thinner bill.

Stan's Notes: Smallest bird in North America. Common in open forests and brushy areas in lower elevations of Idaho. A relatively quiet bird, it will come to nectar feeders. During breeding season, males can be heard zinging around while displaying for females. Females are hard to distinguish from other female hummingbirds. Often builds nest on branches of pine trees. Juvenile males obtain a partial throat patch by autumn of their first year.

male

female

BROAD-TAILED HUMMINGBIRD
Selasphorus platycercus

Size: 4" (10 cm)

Male: Tiny iridescent green bird with black throat patch (gorget) that reflects rosy red in sunlight. Wings and part of the back are green. White chest.

Female: same as male, but lacking the throat patch, much more green on back, tan flanks

Juvenile: similar to female

Nest: cup; female builds; 1-2 broods per year

Eggs: 1-3; white without markings

Incubation: 12-14 days; female incubates

Fledging: 20-22 days; female feeds young

Migration: complete, to Central and South America

Food: nectar, insects; will come to nectar feeders

Compare: Calliope Hummingbird (pg. 119) is smaller and has wing tips that reach to tip of tail. Slightly larger than Rufous Hummingbird (pg. 237), lacking the characteristic burnt orange color of the Rufous.

Stan's Notes: Hummingbirds are the only birds with the ability to fly backward. Doesn't sing. Will chatter or buzz to communicate. Wing beats produce a whistle, almost like a tiny ringing bell. Heart pumps an incredible 1,260 beats per minute. Weighing just 2 to 3 gm, it takes about five average-sized hummingbirds to equal the weight of one chickadee. Male performs a spectacular pendulum-like flight over the perched female. After mating, female builds nest and raises young without any help from her mate. Constructs a soft flexible nest that expands to accommodate the growing young.

male

female

SUMMER

VIOLET-GREEN SWALLOW
Tachycineta thalassina

Size: 5¼" (13.5 cm)

Male: Dull emerald green crown, nape and back. Violet blue wings and tail. White chest and belly. White cheeks with white extending above the eyes. Wings extend beyond the tail when perching.

Female: same as male, only duller

Juvenile: similar to adult of the same sex

Nest: cavity; the female and male build; 1 brood per year

Eggs: 4-6; pale white with brown markings

Incubation: 13-14 days; female incubates

Fledging: 18-24 days; female and male feed young

Migration: complete, to Central and South America

Food: insects

Compare: Similar size as the Cliff Swallow (pg. 81), which has a distinctive tan-to-rust pattern on the head. Barn Swallow (pg. 55) has a distinctive, deeply forked tail. Tree Swallow (pg. 53) is mostly a deep blue, lacking any emerald green of the Violet-green Swallow.

Stan's Notes: A solitary nester in tree cavities, but rarely beneath cliff overhangs, unlike the colony-nesting Cliff Swallow. Like Tree Swallows, can be attracted with a nest box. Will search for miles for errant feathers to line its nest. A short tail with wing tips extending beyond the end of the tail when perching. Returns to Idaho in late April and begins nesting in May. Young often leave nest by June.

GREEN-TAILED TOWHEE
Pipilo chlorurus

Size: 7¼" (18.5 cm)

Male: A unique yellowish green back, wings and tail. Dark gray chest and face. Bright white throat with black stripes. Rusty red crown.

Female: same as male

Juvenile: olive green with heavy streaking on breast and belly, lacks crown and throat markings of adult

Nest: cup; the female and male build; 1-2 broods per year

Eggs: 3-5; white with brown markings

Incubation: 12-14 days; female and male incubate

Fledging: 10-14 days; female and male feed young

Migration: complete, to Mexico and Central America

Food: insects, seeds, fruit

Compare: Spotted Towhee (pg. 7) is black with rusty sides, appearing nothing like Green-tailed Towhee. Green-tailed's unusual color, short wings, long tail and large bill make it an easy bird to identify.

Stan's Notes: A common bird of shrubby hillsides and sagebrush mountain slopes as high as 7,000 feet (2,150 m). Arrives in Idaho in May. Begins breeding in June. Like other towhees, the Green-tailed searches for insects and seeds by taking a little jump forward while kicking backward with both feet. Known for scurrying away from trouble by jumping to ground without opening wings, and then running across the ground.

LEWIS'S WOODPECKER
Melanerpes lewis

Size: 10¾" (27.5 cm)

Male: Dull green head and back. Distinctive gray collar and breast. Deep red face and a light red belly.

Female: same as male

Juvenile: similar to adult, with a brown head, lacking the red face

Nest: cavity; the male and female build; 1 brood per year

Eggs: 4-8; white without markings

Incubation: 13-14 days; female and male incubate

Fledging: 28-34 days; female and male feed young

Migration: complete, to southern states and Mexico, small percentage non-migrator in Idaho

Food: insects, nuts, seeds, berries

Compare: Red-naped Sapsucker (pg. 29) has a black-and-white pattern on the back and much more red on the head. Male Williamson's Sapsucker (pg. 31) has a black back and large white wing patches.

Stan's Notes: Large and handsome woodpecker of western states. First collected and named in 1806 by Lewis and Clark in Idaho. During breeding season, it feeds exclusively on insects rather than grubs, like other woodpeckers. Prefers open pine forests and areas with recent forest fires. Excavates in dead or soft wood. Uses same cavity year after year. Tends to mate for long term. Moves around in winter to search for food such as pine nuts (seeds).

male

female pg. 139

WOOD DUCK
Aix sponsa

YEAR-ROUND
SUMMER

Size: 17-20" (43-50 cm)

Male: A small, highly ornamented dabbling duck with a green head and crest patterned with white and black. A rusty chest, white belly and red eyes.

Female: brown, similar size and shape as male, has bright white eye-ring and a not-so-obvious crest, blue patch on wing often hidden

Juvenile: same as female

Nest: cavity; female lines old woodpecker cavity; 1 brood per year

Eggs: 10-15; creamy white without markings

Incubation: 28-36 days; female incubates

Fledging: 56-68 days; female teaches young to feed

Migration: complete, to southern states, partial to non-migrator in the northern Panhandle

Food: aquatic insects, plants, seeds

Compare: More colorful than male Green-winged Teal (pg. 129). Smaller than the male Shoveler (pg. 231) and lacks the long wide bill.

Stan's Notes: A common duck of quiet, shallow backwater ponds. Nearly extinct around 1900 due to overhunting, but is doing well now. Nests in an old woodpecker hole or uses a nesting box. Often seen flying deep in forest or perched high on tree branches. Female takes to flight with a loud squealing call and enters nest cavity from full flight. Young stay in nest cavity 24 hours after hatching, then jump from up to 30 feet (9 m) to the ground or water to follow their mother, never returning to the nest.

male

female pg. 143

NORTHERN SHOVELER
Anas clypeata

MIGRATION
SUMMER

Size: 20" (50 cm)

Male: Medium-sized duck with iridescent green head, rusty sides and white breast. Has an extraordinarily large spoon-shaped bill that is almost always held pointed toward water.

Female: same spoon-shaped bill, brown and black all over and blue wing patch

Juvenile: same as female

Nest: ground; female builds; 1 brood per year

Eggs: 9-12; olive without markings

Incubation: 22-25 days; female incubates

Fledging: 30-60 days; female leads young to food

Migration: complete, to southern states, Mexico and Central America

Food: aquatic insects, plants

Compare: Similar to the male Mallard (pg. 235), but Shoveler has a large, characteristic spoon-shaped bill. Larger than male Wood Duck (pg. 229) and lacks the Wood Duck's crest. Shares the cinnamon-colored sides of male Cinnamon Teal (pg. 133), but is larger.

Stan's Notes: One of several species of shoveler, so called because of the peculiarly shaped bill. The Northern Shoveler is the only species of these ducks in North America. Seen in small flocks of five to ten, swimming low in water with large bills always pointed toward the water, as if they're too heavy to lift. Feeds primarily by filtering tiny plants and insects from the water's surface with bill.

female pg. 251

male

COMMON MERGANSER
Mergus merganser

YEAR-ROUND

Size: 27" (69 cm)

Male: Long, thin, duck-like bird with green head, a black back, and white sides, breast and neck. Has a long, pointed orange bill. Often appears to be black and white in poor light.

Female: same size and shape as the male, but with a rust red head, ragged "hair" on head, gray body with white chest and chin, and long, pointed orange bill

Juvenile: same as female

Nest: cavity; female lines old woodpecker cavity; 1 brood per year

Eggs: 9-11; ivory without markings

Incubation: 28-33 days; female incubates

Fledging: 70-80 days; female feeds young

Migration: partial migrator to non-migrator in Idaho

Food: small fish, aquatic insects

Compare: Similar size as male Mallard (pg. 235), but male Common Merganser has a black back, bright white sides and a long pointed bill.

Stan's Notes: Can be found on just about any open water in the winter, but more common along rivers than lakes. Mergansers are shallow water divers that feed on fish in no more than 10 to 15 feet (3 to 4.5 m) of water. The bill has a fine serrated-like edge to help catch slippery fish. Females often lay eggs in other merganser nests (egg dumping), resulting in broods of up to 15 young per mother. The male leaves the female as soon as she starts to incubate eggs. Orphans are accepted by other merganser mothers with young.

233

female pg. 161

male

MALLARD
Anas platyrhynchos

YEAR-ROUND

Size: 27-28" (69-71 cm)

Male: Large, bulbous green head, white necklace and rust brown or chestnut-colored chest. A combination of gray and white on sides. Yellow bill. Orange legs and feet.

Female: all brown with orange and black bill, small blue and white wing mark (speculum)

Juvenile: same as female, but with a yellow bill

Nest: ground; female builds; 1 brood per year

Eggs: 7-10; greenish to whitish, unmarked

Incubation: 26-30 days; female incubates

Fledging: 42-52 days; female leads young to food

Migration: partial migrator to non-migrator in Idaho

Food: seeds, plants, aquatic insects; will come to ground feeders offering corn

Compare: The male Northern Shoveler (pg. 231) has a white chest with rust on sides and a dark spoon-shaped bill. Breeding male Northern Pintail (pg. 159) is slightly smaller and has extremely long central tail feathers and a brown head.

Stan's Notes: A familiar duck of lakes and ponds, it's considered a type of dabbling duck, tipping forward in shallow water to feed on aquatic plants on the bottom. The name "Mallard" comes from the Latin *masculus*, meaning "male," referring to the habit of males not taking part in raising ducklings. Black central tail feathers of male curl upward. Both the male and female have white tails and white underwings. Will return to place of birth.

male

female

RUFOUS HUMMINGBIRD
Selasphorus rufus

Size: 3¾" (9.5 cm)

Male: Tiny burnt orange bird with a black throat patch (gorget) that reflects orange-red in sunlight. White chest. Green-to-tan flanks.

Female: same as male, but lacking the throat patch

Juvenile: similar to female

Nest: cup; female builds; 1-2 broods per year

Eggs: 1-3; white without markings

Incubation: 14-17 days; female incubates

Fledging: 21-26 days; female feeds young

Migration: complete, to Central and South America

Food: nectar, insects; will come to nectar feeders

Compare: Unique bird that is identified by the orange (rufous) coloring.

Stan's Notes: One of the smallest birds in the state. A bold, hardy hummer, it is often seen well out of its normal range in the western U.S., showing up all along the East coast. Will visit hummingbird feeders in your yard. Doesn't sing, but will chatter or buzz to communicate. Weighing just 2 to 3 gm, it takes about five average-sized hummingbirds to equal the weight of a single chickadee. Heart pumps an incredible 1,260 beats per minute. Male performs a spectacular pendulum-like flight over the perched female. After mating, the female flies off to build a nest and raise young, without any help from her mate. Constructs a soft flexible nest that expands to accommodate the growing young.

female pg. 277

male

BULLOCK'S ORIOLE
Icterus bullockii

SUMMER

Size: 8" (20 cm)

Male: Bright orange and black bird. Black crown, eye line, nape, chin, wings and back with orange elsewhere. Bold white patch on the wings.

Female: dull yellow overall, pale white belly, white wing bars on gray-to-black wings

Juvenile: similar to female

Nest: pendulous; female and male build; 1 brood per year

Eggs: 4-6; pale white to gray, brown markings

Incubation: 12-14 days; female incubates

Fledging: 12-14 days; female and male feed young

Migration: complete, to Central and South America

Food: insects, berries, nectar; visits nectar feeders

Compare: A handsome bird. Look for male Bullock's bright orange and black markings, and thin black line running through eyes.

Stan's Notes: So closely related to Baltimore Orioles of the eastern U.S., at one time both were considered a single species. Interbreeds with the Baltimore where ranges overlap. Most common in Idaho where cottonwood trees grow alongside rivers and other wetlands. Also found at edges of clearings, in city parks, on farms and along irrigation ditches. Hanging sock-like nest is constructed of plant fibers such as inner bark of junipers and willows. Will incorporate yarn and thread into its nest if offered at the time of nest building.

female pg. 109

male

SUMMER

BLACK-HEADED GROSBEAK
Pheucticus melanocephalus

Size: 8" (20 cm)

Male: Stocky bird with burnt orange chest, neck and rump. Black head, tail and wings with irregular-shaped white wing patches. Large bill with upper bill darker than lower.

Female: appears like an overgrown sparrow, overall brown with lighter-colored chest and belly, bold white eyebrows, large two-toned bill

Juvenile: similar to adult of the same sex

Nest: cup; female builds; 1 brood per year

Eggs: 3-4; pale green or bluish, brown markings

Incubation: 11-13 days; female and male incubate

Fledging: 11-13 days; female and male feed young

Migration: complete, to Mexico, Central America and South America

Food: insects, seeds, fruit

Compare: Same size as the male Evening Grosbeak (pg. 279), but male Black-headed has an orange breast and lacks a yellow belly. Look for its large bicolored bill.

Stan's Notes: A cosmopolitan bird that nests in a wide variety of habitats, seeming to prefer the foothills slightly more than other places. Both males and females sing and aggressively defend their nests against intruders. Song is very similar to the American Robin's and Western Tanager's, making it hard to tell them apart by song. Populations are increasing in Idaho and across the U.S.

male

female

VARIED THRUSH
Ixoreus naevius

YEAR-ROUND
MIGRATION
SUMMER

Size: 9½" (24 cm)

Male: Potbellied robin-like bird with orange eyebrows, chin, breast and wing bars. Head, neck and back are gray to blue. Black breast band and eye mark.

Female: browner version of male, lacking the black breast band

Juvenile: similar to female

Nest: cup; female builds; 1-2 broods per year

Eggs: 3-5; pale blue with brown markings

Incubation: 12-14 days; female incubates

Fledging: 10-15 days; female and male feed young

Migration: partial migrator to non-migrator, to West coast states

Food: insects, fruit

Compare: Similar size and shape as American Robin (pg. 195), but has a warm orange breast, compared with the brick red breast of the Robin. Male Varied Thrush has a distinctive black breast band.

Stan's Notes: An intriguing-looking bird. Nests in Alaska, Canada and the mountains of the U.S. Northwest. Prefers moist coniferous forest. It is most common in dense, older coniferous forests in high elevations. Moves to lower elevations in the winter where it is often seen in towns and orchards and thickets, or migrates to California. Seen in flocks during winter of up to 20 birds. Well known for individual birds to fly eastward in winter, showing up in just about any state, then returning to Idaho and the West coast for breeding.

yellow male

female pg. 73

male

HOUSE FINCH
Carpodacus mexicanus

YEAR-ROUND

Size: 5" (13 cm)

Male: An orange red face, breast and rump, with a brown cap. Brown marking behind eyes. Brown wings streaked with white. A white belly with brown streaks.

Female: brown with a heavily streaked white chest

Juvenile: similar to female

Nest: cup, sometimes in cavities; female builds; 2 broods per year

Eggs: 4-5; pale blue, lightly marked

Incubation: 12-14 days; female incubates

Fledging: 15-19 days; female and male feed young

Migration: non-migrator to partial migrator; will move around to find food

Food: seeds, fruit, leaf buds; will visit seed feeders

Compare: Male Cassin's Finch (pg. 247) is similar, but is a rosy red, unlike the orange red of male House Finch, and lacks a brown cap. Look for the streaked chest and belly, and brown cap of male House Finch.

Stan's Notes: Very social bird. Visits feeders in small flocks. Likes nesting in hanging flower baskets. Incubating female fed by male. Loud, cheerful warbling song. Suffers a fatal eye disease that causes eyes to crust over. Historically it occurred from the Pacific coast to the Rocky Mountains, with a few reaching the eastern side. Birds introduced to Long Island, New York, in the 1940s have populated the entire eastern U.S. Now found all over the U.S. Rarely, some males are yellow (see inset) instead of red, probably due to poor diet.

male

female pg. 91

Carpodacus cassinii

YEAR-ROUND
SUMMER

Size: 6½" (16 cm)

Male: Overall light wash of crimson red with an especially bright red crown. Distinct brown streaks on back and wings. White belly.

Female: overall brown to gray, fine black streaks on the back and wings, heavily streaked white chest and belly

Juvenile: similar to female

Nest: cup; female builds; 1-2 broods per year

Eggs: 3-5; white without markings

Incubation: 12-14 days; female incubates

Fledging: 14-18 days; female and male feed young

Migration: partial migrator to non-migrator; will move around to find food

Food: seeds, insects, fruits, berries; will visit seed feeders

Compare: Similar to the male House Finch (pg. 245), which has a brown cap, is heavily streaked on flanks and is orange red, unlike the male Cassin's rosy red. Much redder than Gray-crowned Rosy-Finch (pg. 89).

Stan's Notes: A common mountain finch of coniferous forests. It usually forages for seeds on the ground, but eats evergreen buds and aspen and willow catkins. Breeds in May. A colony nester, depending on the regional food source. The more food available, the larger the colony. Male sings a rapid warble, often imitating other birds such as jays, tanagers and grosbeaks. A cowbird host.

female pg. 273

male

RED CROSSBILL
Loxia curvirostra

YEAR-ROUND

Size: 6½" (16 cm)

Male: Sparrow-sized bird, dirty red to orange with bright red crown and rump. Long, pointed, crossed bill. Dark brown wings and a short dark brown tail.

Female: pale yellow chest, light gray throat patch, a crossed bill, dark brown wings and tail

Juvenile: streaked with tinges of yellow, bill gradually crosses about two weeks after fledging

Nest: cup; female builds; 1 brood per year

Eggs: 3-4; bluish white with brown markings

Incubation: 14-18 days; female incubates

Fledging: 16-20 days; female and male feed young

Migration: non-migrator to irruptive; moves around the state in winter to find food

Food: seeds, leaf buds; comes to seed feeders

Compare: Larger than the male House Finch (pg. 245) and has a unique crossed bill.

Stan's Notes: The long crossed bill is adapted for extracting seeds from pine and spruce cones, its favorite food. Often dangles upside down like a parrot to reach cones. Also seen on the ground where it eats grit, which helps digest food. Plumage can be highly variable among individuals. Nests in low elevation coniferous forests. While it is a resident nester, migrating crossbills from farther north move into Idaho during winter, searching for food, swelling populations. This irruptive behavior makes them common in some winters and scarce in others.

male pg. 233

female

COMMON MERGANSER
Mergus merganser

YEAR-ROUND

Size: 27" (69 cm)

Female: A long, thin, duck-like bird with a rust red head and ragged "hair" on the back of head. Gray body with white chest and chin. Long, pointed orange bill.

Male: same size and shape as the female, but with a green head, black back, white sides and chest, and long, pointed orange bill

Juvenile: same as female

Nest: cavity; female lines old woodpecker cavity; 1 brood per year

Eggs: 9-11; ivory without markings

Incubation: 28-33 days; female incubates

Fledging: 70-80 days; female feeds young

Migration: partial migrator to non-migrator in Idaho

Food: small fish, aquatic insects

Compare: Hard to confuse with other birds. Look for ragged "hair" on back of a red head, a long, pointed orange bill, white chest and chin.

Stan's Notes: Can be found on just about any open water in the winter, but more common along rivers than lakes. Mergansers are shallow water divers that feed on fish in no more than 10 to 15 feet (3 to 4.5 m) of water. The bill has a fine serrated-like edge to help catch slippery fish. Females often lay eggs in other merganser nests (egg dumping), resulting in broods of up to 15 young per mother. The male leaves the female as soon as she starts to incubate eggs. Orphans are accepted by other merganser mothers with young.

winter

juvenile

breeding

YEAR-ROUND
MIGRATION
WINTER

Size: 19" (48 cm); up to 4-foot wingspan

Male: A white bird with gray wings, black wing tips spotted with white, and a white tail, as seen in flight. Yellow bill with a black ring near tip. Yellowish legs and feet. Winter or non-breeding adult has a speckled brown back of head and nape of neck.

Female: same as male

Juvenile: mostly gray version of adult, has dark band at end of tail

Nest: ground; the female and male build; 1 brood per year

Eggs: 2-4; off-white with brown markings

Incubation: 20-21 days; female and male incubate

Fledging: 20-40 days; female and male feed young

Migration: partial migrator to complete, along western coastal U.S., to southern states and Mexico

Food: insects, fish; scavenges for food

Compare: Smaller than the California Gull (pg. 255), which has a larger bill with a red and black mark near the tip, and dark eyes, compared with the Ring-billed's light-colored eyes.

Stan's Notes: A common gull of garbage dumps and parking lots. Nests in the southern third of Idaho, sometimes nesting in mixed colonies with other gull species. Defends a small area around nest, usually a few feet. A three-year gull with a new, different plumage in each of the first three autumns. Attains ring on bill after the first winter. Doesn't attain adult plumage until the third year.

winter

breeding

CALIFORNIA GULL
Larus californicus

Size: 21" (53 cm)

Male: White bird with gray wings and black wing tips. A red and black mark on tip of yellow bill. Red ring around dark eyes. Winter or non-breeding adult has brown streaks on back of head and nape of neck.

Female: same as male

Juvenile: all brown for the first two years, similar to adult by third year

Nest: ground; the female and male build; 1 brood per year

Eggs: 2-5; pale brown or olive, brown markings

Incubation: 24-26 days; female and male incubate

Fledging: 40-45 days; female and male feed young

Migration: partial migrator to complete, along western coastal U.S. and Mexico

Food: insects, seeds, mammals

Compare: Larger than the Ring-billed Gull (pg. 253), which lacks California Gull's dark eyes and red mark on bill.

Stan's Notes: Famed gull species that saved crops from an over-population of grasshoppers in 1848 and inspired gull monuments in Salt Lake City. A four-year gull, the first two years appearing nearly all brown. Third year is similar to the winter adult. Usually doesn't nest until the fourth year, when it obtains adult plumage. Nests in large colonies (up to 1,000 nests) in the southern half of Idaho. Named for its usual winter sites along the California coast.

blue morph

juvenile

white morph

in flight

MIGRATION

SNOW GOOSE
Chen caerulescens

Size: 25-38" (63-96 cm)

Male: A mostly white goose with varying patches of black and brown. Black wing tips. Pink bill and legs. Some birds are grayish with a white head.

Female: same as male

Juvenile: overall dull gray with a dark bill

Nest: ground; female builds; 1 brood per year

Eggs: 3-5; white without markings

Incubation: 23-25 days; female incubates

Fledging: 45-49 days; female and male teach young to feed

Migration: complete, to southern states, New Mexico, California and Mexico

Food: aquatic insects and plants

Compare: Smaller than the Canada Goose (pg. 213), lacking a black neck and white chin strap. Much smaller than American White Pelican (pg. 261), sharing the black wing tips but lacking the enormous bill.

Stan's Notes: Two color morphs. The more common white morph is pure white with black wing tips. Gray morph is often called blue, with a white head, gray chest and back, and pink bill and legs. Has a thick serrated bill for pulling up plants. Breeds in large colonies on the tundra of northern Canada. Females don't breed until they are 2 to 3 years old. Older females produce more eggs and are more successful than the younger females. Seen by the tens of thousands during migration. Often associated with Sandhill Cranes.

GREAT EGRET
Ardea alba

MIGRATION
SUMMER

Size: 38" (96 cm)

Male: Tall, thin, elegant all-white bird with long, pointed yellow bill. Black stilt-like legs and black feet.

Female: same as male

Juvenile: same as adult

Nest: platform; male and female build; 1 brood per year

Eggs: 2-3; light blue without markings

Incubation: 23-26 days; female and male incubate

Fledging: 43-49 days; female and male feed young

Migration: complete, to southern states, Mexico and Central America

Food: fish, aquatic insects, frogs, crayfish

Compare: The Great Blue Heron (pg. 217) is larger in size, but has a similar shape.

Stan's Notes: A tall and stately bird, the Great Egret slowly stalks shallow wetlands looking for small fish to spear with its long sharp bill. Nests in colonies of up to 100 birds. Now protected, they were hunted to near extinction in the 1800s and early 1900s for their long white plumage. The name "Egret" came from the French word *aigrette*, which means "ornamental tufts of plumes." The plumes grow near the tail during breeding season.

chick-feeding
adult

AMERICAN WHITE PELICAN
Pelecanus erythrorhynchos

Size: 62" (158 cm); up to 9-foot wingspan

Male: A large white bird with black wing tips that extend partially down the trailing edge of wings. A white or pale yellow crown. Bright yellow bill, legs and feet. Breeding adult has a bright orange bill and legs. An adult that is feeding chicks (chick-feeding adult) has a gray-black crown.

Female: same as male

Juvenile: duller white with brownish head and neck

Nest: ground, a scraped-out depression rimmed with dirt; female and male build; 1 brood per year

Eggs: 1-3; white without markings

Incubation: 29-36 days; male and female incubate

Fledging: 60-70 days; female and male feed young

Migration: complete, Central and South America

Food: fish

Compare: Snow Goose (pg. 257) is much smaller and lacks the Pelican's enormous bill.

Stan's Notes: Frequently seen in large groups on the larger lakes and reservoirs of Idaho during migration and summer. They feed by simultaneously dipping their bills into water to scoop up fish. They don't dive in water to catch fish, like coastal Brown Pelicans. Bills and legs of breeding adults turn deep orange. Breeding adults usually also grow a flat fibrous plate in the middle of the upper mandible. This plate drops off after eggs have hatched. They fly in a large V, often gliding with long wings, then all flapping together.

female

male

WILSON'S WARBLER
Wilsonia pusilla

Size: 4¾" (12 cm)

Male: Dull yellow upper and bright yellow lower. Distinctive black cap. Large black eyes and small thin bill.

Female: same as male, but lacking the black cap

Juvenile: similar to female

Nest: cup; female builds; 1 brood per year

Eggs: 4-6; white with brown markings

Incubation: 10-13 days; female incubates

Fledging: 8-11 days; female and male feed young

Migration: complete, to coastal Texas, Central America and Mexico

Food: insects

Compare: Yellow Warbler (pg. 271) is brighter yellow with orange streaking on the male's chest. Male American Goldfinch (pg. 265) has a black forehead and black wings. Common Yellowthroat (pg. 267) has a very distinctive black mask.

Stan's Notes: A widespread warbler of low to mid-level elevations. Can be found near water in willow and alder thickets. Its all-insect diet makes it one of the top insect-eating birds in the state. Often flicks tail and spreads wings when hopping among thick shrubs, looking for insects. Females often mate with males that have the best territories and that might already have mates (polygyny).

male

winter male

female

AMERICAN GOLDFINCH
Carduelis tristis

YEAR-ROUND

Size: 5" (13 cm)

Male: A perky yellow bird with a black patch on forehead. Black tail with conspicuous white rump. Black wings with white wing bars. No marking on the chest. Dramatic change in color during winter, similar to female.

Female: dull olive yellow without a black forehead, with brown wings and a white rump

Juvenile: same as female

Nest: cup; female builds; 1 brood per year

Eggs: 4-6; pale blue without markings

Incubation: 10-12 days; female incubates

Fledging: 11-17 days; female and male feed young

Migration: partial migrator to non-migrator; flocks of up to 20 move around North America

Food: seeds, insects; will come to seed feeders

Compare: The Pine Siskin (pg. 71) and female House Finch (pg. 73) have streaked breasts. Male Yellow Warbler (pg. 271) is all yellow with orange streaks on the chest. Male Wilson's Warbler (pg. 263) lacks black wings.

Stan's Notes: Most often found in open fields, scrubby areas and woodlands. Often called Wild Canary. A feeder bird that enjoys Nyger Thistle. Late summer nesting, uses the silky down from wild thistle for nest. Appears roller-coaster-like in flight. Listen for it to twitter during flight. Almost always in small flocks. Moves only far enough south to find food.

SUMMER

COMMON YELLOWTHROAT
Geothlypis trichas

Size: 5" (13 cm)

Male: Olive brown bird with bright yellow throat and breast, a white belly and a distinctive black mask outlined in white. A long, thin, pointed black bill.

Female: same as male, but lacking the black mask

Juvenile: same as female

Nest: cup; female builds; 2 broods per year

Eggs: 3-5; white with brown markings

Incubation: 11-12 days; female incubates

Fledging: 10-11 days; female and male feed young

Migration: complete, to southern states, Mexico and Central America

Food: insects

Compare: Found in a similar habitat as the American Goldfinch (pg. 265), but lacks the male's black forehead and wings. The male Yellow Warbler (pg. 271) has fine orange streaks on chest and lacks the black mask. Yellow-rumped Warbler (pg. 183) has only spots of yellow. Male Wilson's Warbler (pg. 263) lacks the Yellowthroat's black mask.

Stan's Notes: A common warbler of open fields and marshes. Has a cheerful, well-known song, "witchity-witchity-witchity-witchity." The male performs a curious courtship display, bouncing in and out of tall grass while uttering an unusual song. The young remain dependent upon the parents longer than most warblers. A frequent cowbird host.

ORANGE-CROWNED WARBLER
Vermivora celata

SUMMER

Size: 5" (13 cm)

Male: An overall pale yellow bird with a dark line through eyes. Faint streaking on sides and chest. Small thin bill. Tawny orange crown, often invisible.

Female: same as male, but very slightly duller, often indistinguishable in the field

Juvenile: same as adults

Nest: cup; female builds; 1-2 broods per year

Eggs: 3-6; white with brown markings

Incubation: 12-14 days; female incubates

Fledging: 8-10 days; female and male feed young

Migration: complete, to coastal states, Central America and Mexico

Food: insects, fruit, nectar

Compare: Yellow Warbler (pg. 271) is brighter yellow with orange streaking on the male's chest. Wilson's Warbler (pg. 263) is also brighter yellow with a distinct black cap. Common Yellowthroat (pg. 267) has very distinctive black mask.

Stan's Notes: A widespread bird across Idaho. A nesting resident but often seen more during migration, when large groups move together. Builds a bulky, well-concealed cup nest on the ground with the nest rim at ground level. Known to feed at sapsucker taps and drink flower nectar. The orange crown tends to be hidden and is rarely seen in the field. A widespread breeder, from western Texas to Alaska and across Canada.

male

female

SUMMER

YELLOW WARBLER
Dendroica petechia

Size: 5" (13 cm)

Male: Yellow warbler with orange streaks on the chest and belly. Long, pointed dark bill.

Female: same as male, but lacking orange streaking

Juvenile: similar to female, only much duller

Nest: cup; female builds; 1 brood per year

Eggs: 4-5; white with brown markings

Incubation: 11-12 days; female incubates

Fledging: 10-12 days; female and male feed young

Migration: complete, to southern states, Mexico, and Central and South America

Food: insects

Compare: Look for orange streaking on chest of male. Orange-crowned Warbler (pg. 269) is paler yellow. Male American Goldfinch (pg. 265) has black wings and forehead. The female Yellow Warbler is similar to the female American Goldfinch (pg. 265), but lacks white wing bars. Similar to male Wilson's Warbler (pg. 263), which has a black cap, and lacks orange streaks on chest and belly.

Stan's Notes: A widespread and common warbler in Idaho, seen in gardens and shrubby areas near water. It is a prolific insect eater, gleaning small caterpillars and other insects from tree leaves. Male is often seen higher up in trees than the female bird. Female is less conspicuous. Starts to migrate in August and returns in late April. Males arrive a week or two before the females to claim territories. Migrates at night in mixed flocks of warblers. Rests and feeds days.

female

male pg. 249

RED CROSSBILL
Loxia curvirostra

Size: 6½" (16 cm)

Female: A pale yellow-gray sparrow-sized bird with a pale yellow chest and light gray patch on the throat. Long, pointed, crossed bill. Dark brown wings and a short dark brown tail.

Male: dirty red to orange with a bright red crown and rump, a crossed bill, dark brown wings and a short dark brown tail

Juvenile: streaked with tinges of yellow, bill gradually crosses about two weeks after fledging

Nest: cup; female builds; 1 brood per year

Eggs: 3-4; bluish white with brown markings

Incubation: 14-18 days; female incubates

Fledging: 16-20 days; female and male feed young

Migration: non-migrator to irruptive; moves around the state in winter to find food

Food: seeds, leaf buds; comes to seed feeders

Compare: Larger than the female American Goldfinch (pg. 265). Look for the unique crossed bill.

Stan's Notes: The long crossed bill is adapted for extracting seeds from pine and spruce cones, its favorite food. Often dangles upside down like a parrot to reach cones. Also seen on the ground where it eats grit, which helps digest food. Plumage can be highly variable among individuals. Nests in low elevation coniferous forests. While it is a resident nester, migrating crossbills from farther north move into Idaho during winter, searching for food, swelling populations. This irruptive behavior makes them common in some winters and scarce in others.

non-breeding male

breeding male

female

SUMMER

WESTERN TANAGER
Piranga ludoviciana

Size: 7¼" (18.5 cm)

Male: A canary yellow bird with a red head. Black back, tail, wings. One white and one yellow wing bar. Non-breeding lacks the red head.

Female: duller than male, lacking the red head

Juvenile: similar to female

Nest: cup; female builds; 1 brood per year

Eggs: 3-5; light blue with brown markings

Incubation: 11-13 days; female incubates

Fledging: 13-15 days; female and male feed young

Migration: complete, to Mexico and Central America

Food: insects, fruit

Compare: Male American Goldfinch (pg. 265) has a black forehead and lacks the breeding male Tanager's red head. Unique combination of colors makes the male hard to misidentify. Female Bullock's Oriole (pg. 277) lacks the female Tanager's single yellow wing bars.

Stan's Notes: Common throughout Idaho. The male is stunning in its breeding plumage. Feeds mainly on insects such as bees, wasps, grasshoppers and cicadas. Feeds to a lesser degree on fruit. Male will feed the female as she incubates. Female builds a cup nest in a horizontal fork of a coniferous tree, well away from the main trunk, from 20 to 40 feet (6 to 12 m) above ground. The farthest nesting tanager species, reaching far up into Canada's Northwest Territories. An early fall migrant, often seen migrating in late July (when non-breeding males lack red-colored heads). Can be seen in just about any habitat during migration.

male pg. 239

female

BULLOCK'S ORIOLE
Icterus bullockii

SUMMER

Size: 8" (20 cm)

Female: Dull yellow head and chest. Gray-to-black wings with white wing bars. A pale white belly. Gray back, as seen in flight.

Male: bright orange and black, bold white patch on wings

Juvenile: similar to female

Nest: pendulous; female and male build; 1 brood per year

Eggs: 4-6; pale white to gray, brown markings

Incubation: 12-14 days; female incubates

Fledging: 12-14 days; female and male feed young

Migration: complete, to Central and South America

Food: insects, berries, nectar; visits nectar feeders

Compare: Smaller female Western Tanager (pg. 275) has a black back, unlike the female Oriole's gray back. Look for the overall dull yellow and gray appearance of the female Oriole.

Stan's Notes: So closely related to Baltimore Orioles of the eastern U.S., at one time both were considered a single species. Interbreeds with the Baltimore where ranges overlap. Most common in Idaho where cottonwood trees grow alongside rivers and other wetlands. Also found at edges of clearings, in city parks, on farms and along irrigation ditches. Hanging sock-like nest is constructed of plant fibers such as inner bark of junipers and willows. Will incorporate yarn and thread into its nest if offered at the time of nest building.

male

female

YEAR-ROUND

EVENING GROSBEAK
Coccothraustes vespertinus

Size: 8" (20 cm)

Male: A striking bird with a stocky body, a large ivory-to-greenish bill and bright yellow eyebrows. Dirty yellow head, black-and-white wings and tail, and yellow rump and belly.

Female: similar to male, with softer colors and a gray head and throat

Juvenile: same as female, but with a brown bill

Nest: cup; female builds; 1 brood per year

Eggs: 3-4; blue with brown markings

Incubation: 12-14 days; female incubates

Fledging: 13-14 days; female and male feed young

Migration: non-migrator to irruptive; moves around to find food

Food: seeds, insects, fruit; comes to seed feeders

Compare: Larger than its close relative, the American Goldfinch (pg. 265). Look for the dark head with bright yellow eyebrows and the extra-large bill.

Stan's Notes: One of the largest finches. Characteristic undulating finch-like flight. An unusually large bill for cracking seeds, its main food source. Often seen on gravel roads eating gravel, from which it gets minerals, salt and grit to grind the seeds it eats. A year-round resident, it is more obvious during winter because it moves in large flocks, searching for food, often coming to feeders. Sheds the outer layer of its bill in spring, exposing a blue green bill.

WESTERN KINGBIRD
Tyrannus verticalis

Size: 9" (22.5 cm)

Male: Bright yellow belly and yellow under wings. Gray head and chest, often with white chin. Wings and tail are dark gray to nearly black with white outer edges on tail.

Female: same as male

Juvenile: similar to adult, less yellow and more gray

Nest: cup; female and male build; 1 brood a year

Eggs: 3-4; white with brown markings

Incubation: 18-20 days; female incubates

Fledging: 16-18 days; female and male feed young

Migration: complete, to Central America

Food: insects, berries

Compare: The Eastern Kingbird (pg. 189) lacks any yellow of the Western Kingbird. Western Meadowlark (pg. 283) shares the Western Kingbird's yellow belly, but has a distinctive black V-shaped necklace.

Stan's Notes: A bird of open country, often seen sitting on top of the same shrub or fence post. Hunts by watching for insects, such as bees, grasshoppers and crickets, then flying out to catch them and returning to its perch. Parents teach young how to hunt, often bringing wounded insects back to the nest for the young to chase. Returns in April, nest building in May. Often builds nest in the fork of a small single trunk tree. Common throughout, nesting in trees around homesteads and farms.

WESTERN MEADOWLARK
Sturnella neglecta

Size: 9" (22.5 cm)

Male: Heavy-bodied bird with a short tail. Brown back, yellow chest and prominent black V-shaped necklace. White outer tail feathers.

Female: same as male

Juvenile: same as adult

Nest: cup, on the ground in dense cover; female builds; 1-2 broods per year

Eggs: 3-5; white with brown markings

Incubation: 13-15 days; female incubates

Fledging: 11-13 days; female and male feed young

Migration: non-migrator to partial migrator

Food: insects, seeds

Compare: Western Kingbird (pg. 281) shares a yellow belly, but lacks the Meadowlark's distinctive black V-shaped necklace.

Stan's Notes: This bird resides in open country throughout Idaho. Named "Meadowlark" because it's a bird of meadows and sings like the larks of Europe. Best known for its wonderful song. Not a lark family member, it actually belongs to the blackbird family and is related to blackbirds such as Red-wingeds and orioles. Like other members of the blackbird family, the meadowlark catches prey by poking its long thin bill into places such as holes in the ground or in tufts of grass, where insects are hiding. Opening its mouth to create some space, the bird extracts the bugs. Often seen perching on fence posts, it will quickly dive into tall grass when approached. Conspicuous white markings on sides of its very short, stubby tail.

HELPFUL RESOURCES:

Birder's Bug Book, The. Waldbauer, Gilbert. Cambridge: Harvard University Press, 1998.

Birder's Dictionary. Cox, Randall T. Helena, MT: Falcon Press Publishing, 1996.

Birder's Handbook, The. Ehrlich, Paul R., David S. Dobkin and Darryl Wheye. New York: Simon and Schuster, 1988.

Birds Do It, Too: The Amazing Sex Life of Birds. Harrison, Kit and George H. Harrison. Minocqua, WI: Willow Creek Press, 1997.

Birds of Forest, Yard, and Thicket. Eastman, John. Mechanicsburg, PA: Stackpole Books, 1997.

Birds of North America. Kaufman, Kenn. New York: Houghton Mifflin, 2000.

Blackbirds of the Americas. Orians, Gordon H. Seattle: University of Washington Press, 1985.

Cry of the Sandhill Crane, The. Grooms, Steve. Minocqua, WI: NorthWord Press, 1992.

Dictionary of American Bird Names, The. Choate, Ernest A. Boston: Harvard Common Press, 1985.

Everything You Never Learned About Birds. Rupp, Rebecca. Pownal, VT: Storey Publishing, 1997.

Field Guide to the Birds of North America: Third Edition. Washington, DC: National Geographic Society, 1999.

Field Guide to Warblers of North America, A. Dunn, Jon and Kimball Garrett. Boston: Houghton Mifflin, 1997.

Field Guide to Western Birds, A. Peterson, Roger Tory. Boston: Houghton Mifflin, 1998.

Folklore of Birds. Martin, Laura C. Old Saybrook, CT: Globe Pequot Press, 1996.

Guide to Bird Behavior, A: Vol I, II, III. Stokes, Donald and Lillian Stokes. Boston: Little, Brown and Company, 1989.

How Birds Migrate. Kerlinger, Paul. Mechanicsburg, PA: Stackpole Books, 1995.

Lives of Birds, The: Birds of the World and Their Behavior. Short, Lester L. Collingdale, PA: DIANE Publishing, 2000.

Lives of North American Birds. Kaufman, Kenn. Boston: Houghton Mifflin, 1996.

Living on the Wind. Weidensaul, Scott. New York: North Point Press, 2000.

National Audubon Society: North American Birdfeeder Handbook. Burton, Robert. New York: Dorling Kindersley Publishing, 1995.

National Audubon Society: The Sibley Guide to Bird Life and Behavior. Edited by David Allen Sibley, Chris Elphick and John B. Dunning, Jr. New York: Alfred A. Knopf, 2001.

National Audubon Society: The Sibley Guide to Birds. Sibley, David Allen. New York: Alfred A. Knopf, 2000.

Photographic Guide to North American Raptors, A. Wheeler, Brian K. and William S. Clark. New York: Academic Press, 1999.

Secret Lives of Birds, The. Gingras, Pierre. Toronto: Key Porter Books, 1997.

Secrets of the Nest. Dunning, Joan. Boston: Houghton Mifflin, 1994.

Sparrows and Buntings: A Guide to the Sparrows and Buntings of North America and the World. Byers, Clive, Jon Curson and Urban Olsson. New York: Houghton Mifflin, 1995.

Stokes Bluebird Book: The Complete Guide to Attracting Bluebirds. Stokes, Donald and Lillian Stokes. Boston: Little, Brown and Company, 1991.

Stokes Field Guide to Birds: Western Region. Stokes, Donald and Lillian Stokes. Boston: Little, Brown and Company, 1996.

For reporting unusual bird sightings in Idaho or to hear a recording of where birds have been seen, contact:

Northern	Southeastern	Southwestern
208-882-6195	208-236-3337	208-368-6096

WEB PAGES:

The Internet is a valuable place to learn about birds. You may find birding on the Net a fun way to learn more about birds or spend a long winter night. Following are web sites to assist you in your pursuit of birds.

SITE	ADDRESS
American Birding Association	www.americanbirding.org
Cornell Lab of Ornithology	www.birds.cornell.edu
Author Stan Tekiela's home page	www.naturesmart.com

Use the boxes to check the birds you've seen.

ABOUT THE AUTHOR:

Stan Tekiela is a naturalist, author and wildlife photographer with a Bachelor of Science degree in Natural History from the University of Minnesota. He has been a professional naturalist for more than 20 years and is a member of the Minnesota Naturalist Association, Minnesota Ornithologist Union, Outdoor Writers Association of America and Canon Professional Services. Stan actively studies and photographs birds throughout the U.S. He received an Excellence in Interpretation award from the National Association for Interpretation, and a regional award for Commitment to Outdoor Education. A columnist and radio personality, his syndicated column appears in over 20 cities and he can be heard on a number of radio stations. Stan resides in Victoria, Minnesota, with wife Katherine and daughter Abigail. He can be contacted via his web page at www.naturesmart.com.

Stan authors several field guides for other states including guides for birds, birds of prey, reptiles and amphibians, wildflowers and trees.